'I would urge those working in mental health and education to read this book. Ian achieves a rare feat of combining theory, evidence and practical application in an engaging and comprehensive narrative. This book will help many adults support their young people.'

– *Mike Armiger*

'This practical, wide-ranging and engaging book is an excellent resource for teachers, youth workers and parents. Based on evidence and firmly rooted in the experiences of young people and those who support them, *Teen Substance Use, Mental Health and Body Image* provides advice and strategies that will make a positive difference.'

– *Clare Stafford, CEO, The Charlie Waller Memorial Trust*

'An accessible and helpful guide for professionals looking to build skills and knowledge around adolescent wellbeing. As well as detailing best practice examples, Macdonald importantly highlights approaches which although well-intentioned, can potentially create more problems than they solve. Highly recommended reading.'

– *Rick Bradley, Specialist on Adolescent Mental Health and Substance Use*

of related interest

Self-Harm and Eating Disorders in Schools
A Guide to Whole-School Strategies and Practical Support
Pooky Knightsmith
ISBN 978 1 84905 584 0
eISBN 978 1 78450 031 3

Making PSHE Matter
A Practical Guide to Planning and Teaching Creative PSHE in Primary School
Siân Rowland
ISBN 978 1 78592 286 2
eISBN 978 1 78450 590 5

All About Drugs and Young People
Essential Information and Advice for Parents and Professionals
Julian Cohen
ISBN 978 1 84905 427 0
eISBN 978 0 85700 790 2

Horny and Hormonal
Young People, Sex and the Anxieties of Sexuality
Nick Luxmoore
ISBN 978 1 78592 031 8
eISBN 978 1 78450 278 2

The School of Wellbeing
12 Extraordinary Projects Promoting Children and
Young People's Mental Health and Happiness
Jenny Hulme
ISBN 978 1 78592 096 7
eISBN 978 1 78450 359 8

TEEN SUBSTANCE USE, MENTAL HEALTH AND BODY IMAGE

Practical Strategies for Support

IAN MACDONALD

Jessica Kingsley *Publishers*
London and Philadelphia

First published in 2019
by Jessica Kingsley Publishers
73 Collier Street
London N1 9BE, UK
and
400 Market Street, Suite 400
Philadelphia, PA 19106, USA

www.jkp.com

Library of Congress Cataloging in Publication Data
A CIP catalog record for this book is available from the Library of Congress

British Library Cataloguing in Publication Data
A CIP catalogue record for this book is available from the British Library

ISBN 978 1 78592 867 3
eISBN 978 1 78592 868 0

Printed and bound in Great Britain

MIX
Paper from
responsible sources
FSC
www.fsc.org FSC® C013604

For AJM and SJM

Contents

Acknowledgements   8

Preface   9

1. Developing a Whole School Approach Around 'What Works' in
    Mental Health and Drug and Alcohol Prevention   11

2. Bulging at the Seams: Exploring the Modern Policy Context for
    Mental Health and Drug Education and Prevention 25

3. Theoretical Models of Adolescent Health Behaviours
    and Support   43

4. Alcohol, Smoking, Social Norms and Engaging Parents 57

5. Body Image and IPEDs   69

6. Energy Drinks and Smart Drugs 87

7. Cannabis, NPS and Approaches to 'Illicit' Drugs 93

8. Delivering Effective Mental Health and
    Drug Education in School 103

9. Developing Healthy and Positive Coping 123

*Appendix: Organisations Producing Materials and Resources for
Working with Children and Young People on Mental Health and
Drug Use* 131

References 133

Subject Index 137

Author Index 141

Acknowledgements

I would like to offer specific thanks to those who were directly involved in discussions around this book, as well as reviewing early drafts or adding their views to the 'Points for practice' sections at the end of each chapter. These fantastic individuals include Dr Pooky Knightsmith, Mike Armiger, Andre Tomlin, Rick Bradley, Jamlia Boughelaf, Rob Kleiser and Andy Dunne.

I would also like to thank friends and colleagues from the Charlie Waller Memorial Trust, Mentor UK and the Open University who have enriched my experience of working within the fields of young people's health and education. Working closely with these people really adds weight to the phrase 'every day is a school day'. While my passion for promoting evidence-based practice runs throughout each chapter, this isn't at the expense of hearing and experiencing 'what works' in supporting young people's health. So I also need to acknowledge the young people and professionals I have come across in the course of my work, as I have learnt more from those working in the front line than I ever could by just sticking to books. As such, any young person or professional I have come into contact with over the past 20 years working in the field has had some influence on the content of this book – so I offer my thanks to you all!

Finally, the support of family and close friends was essential in me reaching this point. Thanking those close to you can often be an assumed thing, but sometimes it has to be said too – so thank you to them too; you know who you are.

Preface

This book is aimed primarily at those working with children and young people in secondary school settings. However, my own experiences tell me that not all effective health education takes place in these settings. With that in mind, suggestions and practical ideas can be transferred to wider settings where universal staff come into contact with children and young people. The content means that a range of staff within school settings may find it of use, including senior leadership teams, pastoral teams, Personal, Social and Health Education (PSHE) and health education leads, as well as parents and governors. In wider settings, it may also be of interest to youth workers, sports coaches and school nurses. As the content is more relatable to secondary aged pupils, I have used the term 'young people' more frequently than 'children' to reflect this. However, some of the issues discussed do not just magically appear once secondary school age is reached (11 years old and above), so many of the principles will be relevant to some pupils in primary schools too (11 years old and under). It is noticeable within the UK how community services are increasingly being commissioned to deliver elements of health education within schools. This includes school nurses, young person's drug and alcohol services, sexual health services and targeted mental health services. With this in mind, those working within these services may also find the content useful, as well as those who are commissioning these services within Local Authority Public Health Teams as well as Clinical Commissioning Groups (CCGs). Sections of this book are also based on my experiences of writing blog posts and articles for a variety of sources and publications. As such, the process of writing this book has been an almost cathartic exercise in refocusing my own continuing professional development (CPD), and putting many rambling thoughts and experiences I have had over the years into a more coherent and sharable format!

My experiences working within public health, health promotion and higher education have given me a strong appreciation for the need to adopt evidence-informed practice. This ensures any approach adopted is supported by research and gives us confidence that said approach does what it is supposed to do and is safe to do so too. Increasingly, cost effectiveness comes into this decision-making process with minimal funding available for any programmes in both the health and education spheres. In the UK, we need to get better at not only making research more accessible for those working on the front line, but also being clearer on what it means for improving practice. This is something which is improving, with many universities improving their links with schools and community organisations; this now needs to be expanded to continue closing the gap between evidence and practice. With all this in mind, each chapter seeks to have a strong base in evidence and research on 'what works'. You can also find a 'Points for practice' box at the end of most chapters to highlight some key implications. Some of these are in the form of contributions from specialists working in the field, representing schools, targeted services and the research community. I hope these add an extra perspective to what the content of each chapter means to those working 'at the coal face', and gives you some support to reflect on your own practice as well as ideas for moving things forward in your own school or setting. There are also frequent suggestions for ways to bring the ideas presented to life in your setting. In the spirit of a whole settings approach, some of these are aimed at activities for young people, while others relate to staff or parents.

Recent changes within the field have meant that at the time of writing, the Department for Education (DfE) within the UK is consulting on the content of statutory health education for all English schools. Up until now this topic has been known as Personal, Social and Health Education (PSHE – sometimes an extra E is added at the end to incorporate 'economic' education). With this in mind, I have tried to refer to historical points around the subject as being part of 'PSHE', but indications are we will see stronger status for the subject from 2020, possibly under a wider notion of 'health education'. This is to future-proof the content of this book for UK readers as well as those audiences further afield. It is also acknowledging that the evidence bases referred to throughout will need to be applied, regardless of which moniker the subject comes under.

CHAPTER 1

Developing a Whole School Approach Around 'What Works' in Mental Health and Drug and Alcohol Prevention

This chapter will outline the development of a 'whole school approach' as the starting point for effective approaches to mental health and drug and alcohol issues in young people. Each element of this process is highlighted, with detail for some of these discussed in later chapters. Some of the key data we know about youth health behaviours is also highlighted, while acknowledging that many young people and adults over-estimate the numbers of young people engaging in unhealthy or risky behaviours. This is particularly important given the UK government's recent green paper on children and young people's mental health (Department of Health and Department for Education, 2017), which identifies a clear role for schools in supporting the mental health of pupils. Following on from the earlier Future in Mind strategy document (Department of Health, 2015) around the organising and commissioning of child and adolescent mental health services (CAMHS), the key recommendations of this green paper included:

- A mental health lead to be nominated in every school by 2025 (to be a member of a school's senior leadership team)

- Mental health support teams working directly with schools, including designated leads to act as bridges to specialist services

- Shorter waiting times in accessing specialist support.

In addition, some wider proposals were included to help underpin these recommendations including:

- Increased understanding of the role of social media and the internet on young people's mental health and wellbeing – including a report by the Chief Medical Officer in England

- Research into family support to better understand the role of the family in supporting young people's mental health

- Research into prevention, including an expert group looking into current evidence and research gaps.

Both the schools green paper and Future in Mind have challenged all professionals working with children and young people to think and work differently regarding how their mental health is supported. While health education approaches are tackled in more detail in later chapters, the importance of evidence-based interventions is discussed here, including mindfulness, counselling and other more targeted interventions. Key considerations around the evidence supporting their effectiveness is highlighted too.

Developing a 'whole school approach'

The notion of a whole school approach is something which had a lot of support through the old National Healthy Schools Programme prior to 2010. Since then, local variations of this programme have sought to maintain it as a high priority – albeit without a national policy keeping it high on the agenda. The basic premise is supported by the World Health Organization's concept of a 'whole setting approach' – this promotes the idea that creating healthy communities requires different elements of policy to be in alignment. So as well as health, policies covering education, employment, housing, leisure or the environment also need to take account of how they all impact on health and wellbeing. Within a school environment this is summarised using the components in Figure 1.1.

Figure 1.1: The whole school approach

ACTIVITY

In a staff meeting, have sheets of flipchart paper around the room titled with each element of the whole school approach. Staff can then contribute their own ideas on how each element can be improved by highlighting what the school already does well, as well as 'it would be better if...' These sheets can be left up in a staff area for a week or so to capture thoughts over a period of time.

Leadership and management is purposely at the centre of this model, driven by the fact that without support from senior leaders within a school, long-term change is unlikely to happen. Recent government policy announcements are likely to help this to some extent, with the stated wish for all schools to have a designated mental health lead by 2025. Most importantly, this lead should be a member of the senior leadership team within a school. The role of governors is also important in this element, as without that buy-in at a governance level, a change of head teacher can bring in different perspectives and priorities. The use of data on pupil health behaviours is particularly useful in putting the case forward for senior leaders to invest in a whole school approach to health and wellbeing.

Curriculum is another area being positively influenced by changing government policy in England and Wales. Up until now, PSHE has been a 'recommended' area of the curriculum for schools to focus on. Some statutory elements are present in other areas of the curriculum such as science, but these fall well short of a comprehensive programme highlighted by the PSHE Association and others. We are, however, moving towards a statutory footing for relationship and sex education within a wider programme of health education, which would strengthen this area of the whole school approach nationally. Chapter 8 specifically covers the implications of this and recommendations for adopting best practice.

Parents and carers have an essential role in young people's wellbeing. As such, their views as well as their support needs need to be given consideration. Any approach taken in school can be maximised, or conversely undermined, according to parental influence and attitudes. With this in mind, effective two-way communication between school and home is required, with elements of this covered in later chapters (Chapter 4 has a specific example around alcohol education and information).

Staff development (and wellbeing) is essential if schools are to maintain standards of working in line with best practice – both in terms of pastoral support, school policy implementation, and the planning and delivery of health education. A big gap which will need to be plugged before 2020 is the fact that teacher training has no requirements for health topics as part of gaining qualified teacher status. There are some excellent examples of some initial teacher training providers moving towards this which is great to see, but the majority of staff within schools will need to access this via 'on the job' training. The government commitment for schools in England to receive free Youth Mental Health First Aid training is again admirable, but looks like being limited to one member of staff per school, and focusing on pastoral support and not necessarily delivery of health education. This latter component is covered in detail in Chapter 8, as without effective models of health education, the system is one which is too reactive in nature and chasing its own tail. While improved mental health awareness among school staff is likely to have a wider impact not just on mental illness but also on supporting other risky behaviours like drug use and risky sexual behaviours, it also needs to be acknowledged that young people may not choose that person to disclose to. This therefore raises the further point of finding ways to support staff to feel more confident when a young person chooses them to be the one they trust to tell about their worries. *Staff wellbeing* is so easy to overlook. Yet many schools and colleges who have sought to implement a comprehensive whole school approach often tell me 'we should have started with staff wellbeing'. This element needs to acknowledge the essential role that staff play in the wellbeing of pupils, and that therefore a healthy workforce is more likely to be able to support a healthy school community.

Pupil voice should include, but *has* to go beyond, the role of school councils. The pastoral and educational needs of all pupils need to be reflected in how they receive health education and health support within school. The potential for young people to shape provision is exemplified by HeadStart areas across England, where the delivery of mental health support in their communities is co-produced by young people, schools and professionals (among others). These programmes have been devised to specifically support schools and local communities in improving the mental health and wellbeing of young people aged 10–16. Toolkits produced by these teams, Young Minds and the Anna Freud Centre in particular, are good starting points for schools in planning for meaningful consultation with their pupils.

Targeted support is something which is undergoing change nationally. The Future in Mind report highlighted the limitations of the system we have been operating in up until now, acknowledging the growing chasm between health and education professionals in their views on their roles and responsibilities in supporting child mental health. Future in Mind has prompted local areas to develop their own Local Transformation Plans (LTPs) to outline how support for the mental health of children and young people will be changed at local levels. The main focus of this should be putting the needs of young people and their families at the centre of any support offer, rather than expecting them to fit around the model of support. An important recognition of this has been that most (not all) young people want to be seen by professionals in places they feel comfortable in, with school being a major one of those. This shouldn't mean schools are delivering that support, just offering a space for that support to take place. So schools and other organisations can now be asking themselves whether they have the contacts and working agreements in place to support this process, as well as what is offered at a much lower level to support those young people who are struggling but not in need of specialist support. Chapter 9 explores some of those key skills and strategies which can be adopted within the universal workforce – including school staff, youth workers, school nurses, early help services and others.

Ethos and environment need clear policy to be a clear driver for how a school or organisation approaches the support for young people and staff. This should be a working document and not just one gathering dust on a shelf – or virtual shelf! – which has buy-in from leadership, staff, pupils and parents. It should clearly outline how elements of the whole school approach are supported within school, and what those elements look like. The Charlie Waller Memorial Trust has a useful template for adopting a mental health and wellbeing policy in school (see the list of resources given in the appendix).

Monitoring progress has a key role in terms of finding effective ways to measure the effectiveness of any approach. This doesn't just mean the numbers who have sat through a lesson on mental health or drug use, as that tells us little about the quality of that delivery or how it has impacted on behaviour and attitudes of pupils. With this in mind, simple pre and post-delivery (or intervention) measures can be sought using school-level surveys to measure the changes in attitudes or behaviour over time. While we need to be aware that many other things outside of a school's control can influence these behaviours and attitudes towards mental health and drug use, a semi-regular monitoring process can give an indication of whether an approach is having the intended impact or not.

Mental wellbeing, mental health or mental illness?

There are occasions where, especially in conversation, we can use these three terms interchangeably. Indeed, young people themselves often prefer to use the term 'wellbeing' rather than 'mental health' as it feels easier to engage with. In itself, this fact suggests there is still some level of stigma amongst the younger generation around the term 'mental health' and the implications of using it. This should prompt us to consider the need to appreciate not only the differences between these terms, but more importantly how this impacts on how others engage with them. A useful example is in how we treat the term 'depression'. This is a term we may be likely to hear over the course of a working week in relation to young people, parents and carers, or even colleagues. Yet when we do hear it, or even use it ourselves, are we clear on what is meant by it? On the one hand it is great that society is starting to use terms like this in everyday communication as it shows the stigma associated with mental illness is being chipped away and this is something to be applauded. On the other hand, is 'depression' almost being used too loosely, to describe a temporary drop in mood (linked to wellbeing) rather than describing how someone has been feeling for weeks or even months (linked to mental illness)? This is really important as it influences how we are likely to respond and interact with that person – and we need to know that it is OK to ask exactly what they do mean. If they are describing a temporary drop in mood then we can reinforce the fact that it is OK to experience different mood states, as long as they don't occur too frequently or be too long lasting. If they are describing a more clinical state including frequent or longer-lasting drops in mood, then we may be acknowledging how hard it would be for them to admit to that, as well as offering support, hope and onward referral if required.

The Centre for Longitudinal Studies at University College London (2016) has sought to make a clearer distinction between 'mental illness' and 'wellbeing', as highlighted in Figure 1.2 (a colour version is available via their website). While this may seem a little pedantic to some, this representation helps us appreciate that while there is a cross-over between the two terms, some things are more strongly related with mental ill health than wellbeing, and vice versa. We can see that factors associated with mental illness are more likely to be things which may already be present in a young person's life by the time they start attending a school, while things associated with wellbeing arguably have the potential to be learnt and influenced by school environments. In many ways we can see the things associated with wellbeing as protective factors against mental illness. This is a key point to make as it can shift our thinking on child mental health away from one based on avoiding poor mental health to one focused on promoting positive mental health.

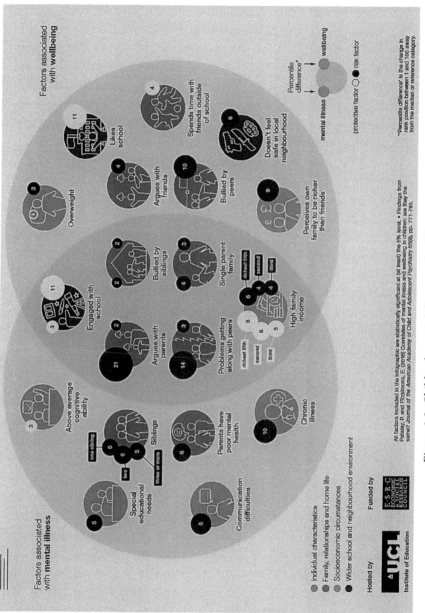

Figure 1.2: Children's mental illness and wellbeing at age 11
Source: Centre for Longitudinal Studies (2016)

What we know about young people's health behaviours

Chapters 4 and 7 look specifically at alcohol and wider substance use among young people, but suffice to say we know that young people tend to over-estimate the numbers of their peers adopting these behaviours (NHS Digital, 2017). This means in wider society we can have a misperception of the prevalence of young people using drugs and alcohol. This can be further skewed by how drug issues are reported in the media, and presented in wider youth culture from film and television to music and YouTubers. The data we do have is often quoted from the 'Smoking, drinking and drug use among young people' survey published via NHS Digital. This survey covers a large sample of young people from age 11 to 15, and asks a range of questions not only around what substances young people use, but also how often, how much, how they got hold of it and their perceptions of them. It has recently gone from being delivered annually to bi-annually, but still represents a string indicator of not only what young people may be doing at a given snapshot in time, but more importantly how trends may change over time. While this data is used extensively to inform planning at local and national levels, it is under-used in producing an evidence-based approach to PSHE and health education. This is understandable given the non-statutory status of health education in England up until now and is something we hope improves post 2020 when health education has its place in the curriculum. Wider promotion by policy makers at national level needs to be underpinned by local education and health professionals too. As an independent charity, Mentor UK regularly produces briefings and specific summaries of this data which schools should find useful, with Public Health England enabling open access to the raw data and visualisations around it and other local datasets through their 'Fingertips' web portal. You can explore this useful tool at https://fingertips.phe.org.uk.

The data referred to here and in subsequent chapters is therefore aimed at supporting those working with young people to gain a wider and more accurate view of the prevalence of alcohol and drug use among young people, as well as highlighting some key trends. If you are lucky, your local authority may still be delivering their own localised version of some national surveys with similar questions. This local data should ideally be the first port of call for PSHE and health education leads looking for data, as the local nature of it will chime more positively with young people, who are more likely to invest in information relative to them rather than someone at the other end of the country.

> ## Young people's health behaviours – what we know
>
> - Numbers of young people drinking have steadily been declining, although those who do drink are drinking more. This has implications for specific support for those young people and early intervention programmes outside of PSHE and health education.
>
> - Despite media representations, the numbers of young people using novel psychoactive substances (NPS, which used to be known as 'legal highs') have been consistently low, with more using in the 16–24 age group as shown through the Crime Survey for England and Wales.
>
> - Cannabis remains the most used illicit substance, and is also the most common substance young people seek support for after alcohol.
>
> - The numbers of young people who say they cope with poor mental health through self-harm have been steadily increasing. We can assume this is in part due to the removal of stigma around mental health and self-harm, but also impacted in a larger way by increased numbers actually engaging in that behaviour.

Current interventions – are they supported by evidence?

Schools are not only opening up their doors for locally commissioned services to deliver interventions onsite, but they are also developing and commissioning their own. This is encouraging from the perspective of schools knowing the specific issues prevalent in their own population, and seeking to respond to that need in appropriate ways. With this in mind, it is important to ensure those responses are based on effective evidence from a solid research base, rather than anecdotal evidence in isolation or shaky evidence.

Mindfulness

An interesting one to consider here is mindfulness. This is an intervention which at its root seeks to allow us:

> to become more aware of the stream of thoughts and feelings that we experience…and to see how we can become entangled in that stream in ways that are not helpful. (Williams, cited in NHS, 2016)

Mindfulness is recommended by the National Institute for Health and Care Excellence (NICE – the body which makes evidence-based recommendations on health treatments) as a way to prevent depression in people who have had multiple bouts. Mindfulness-based interventions have also been shown to decrease stress, anxiety and improve overall health and wellbeing (Hanratty, 2017). This adds credence to its use in a wider preventative approach to mental ill health. However, it has to be stressed that the majority of the evidence base associated with mindfulness and its benefits is associated with adults, and not young people in a school setting (Hanratty, 2017). Furthermore, this can sometimes be at odds with what some providers may claim about the impact of such interventions, with others concluding:

> …it is important that schools understand that MBIs [mindfulness-based interventions] that are accurately portrayed as making significant differences to a number of outcomes are not necessarily going to make changes on a scale that might be anticipated. It is also worth noting that academic achievement measures did not significantly alter across studies, which is often marketed as one of the downstream effects of MBIs. (McDonald and Tomlin, 2017)

These are key considerations when schools are planning (and paying for) mindfulness-based interventions for their pupils, and reinforce the need for this to be viewed as one part of a wider approach to mental health. To return to the whole school approach, this fits within the targeted support element, and therefore needs to be supported by a wider approach around curriculum, staff training, monitoring and parent support, and not a tick-box, catch-all programme. This isn't meant to be presented in a way to scare school leaders away from adopting these interventions, just to help them become more aware of the limitations of putting all your eggs in one mindfulness-shaped basket and the need to maximise the impact of this by placing it within a wider whole school approach.

Counselling and therapeutic interventions

In response to increases in depression and anxiety diagnoses in young people, a range of therapeutic interventions have been subject to increased scrutiny around what is effective in both preventing and treating mental illness. Just as important in this process is where these interventions should take place. Increases in counselling services in schools have been driven in some places by local commissioning of services, and in others by schools responding to identified need through buying in services themselves. This complicated funding pattern has been impacted by changes in funding and commissioning arrangements in different areas of the country, as well as changes in school governance and organisation through the UK government schools' academy programme. This latter factor is particularly prevalent in secondary education, with more secondary schools converting to academy status since 2010. The knock-on effect is the financial autonomy from local authorities which further impacts on perceived access to services and local funding. This all adds to the importance of any interventions around young people's mental health being supported by robust evidence on its effectiveness within school settings.

Guidance from the Department for Education (2015) has helped schools in the planning of school-based counselling services in response to the increased need. Some evidence has shown initial success in school-based prevention programmes for things like anxiety and low mood (Stallard et al., 2015), although the long-term impact and therefore cost effectiveness of these approaches has subsequently been questioned (Underwood, 2016). Wider systematic reviews (a research method considered to be of high quality) have also suggested that school-based prevention programmes have small effects on depression and anxiety (Werner-Seidler et al., 2017), while also acknowledging the potential for schools to contribute to relieving the wider burden of child mental illness. Interestingly, especially with regard to the negative view of the internet in youth mental health, some evidence suggests online interventions can have positive benefits in preventing depression (Perry *et al.*, 2017). Many areas are now including the provision of online support for youth mental health as part of their CAMHS commissioning contracts, with many already up and running. Again, this brings us back to the need for a whole school approach to ensure the best use of these services. Effective PSHE and health education can help promote positive mental health and coping strategies. Alongside this, effective staff training can ensure timely responses and *appropriate* referral to onward counselling and other services. Most importantly an effective whole school approach will also support earlier disclosure of young people when they are struggling, rather than issues only becoming known at points of crisis.

Involving young people in any intervention or prevention activity is essential if it is to be successful. An example of this has been through the funding of HeadStart programmes in ten areas across England, which are aimed at improving the mental health and wellbeing of young people aged 10–16. Some of the key benefits of how this approach is helping young people from these areas include:

- Support when experiencing extreme emotions, arguments with peers, bereavement, academic pressures and family strain

- A positive awareness of potential coping mechanisms

- A recognition of positive changes as a result of having someone to talk to and turn to for simple advice. (Stapley, 2018)

The last two points are of particular importance for schools and universal services, where young people who are experiencing initial instances of poor mental health, but not yet a mental illness, find accessing simple advice and someone to listen to as key elements in them developing positive coping strategies to help manage when they don't feel great. This is acknowledged elsewhere (Knightsmith, 2015) and explored in greater detail in Chapter 3. In practice, it means that some young people do not want, and are therefore unlikely to engage with, a focused therapeutic intervention. This is where lower-level and less intensive approaches can be useful in the first instance prior to any requirements for more in-depth counselling. This is explored in more detail in Chapter 9.

POINTS FOR PRACTICE

- Adopting a whole school approach to health and wellbeing will ensure a focused and sustainable approach to embed across the school community.

- We need to be clear about some of the distinctions between wellbeing, mental health and mental illness.

- Where possible, schools need to be supported in identifying evidence-based practice – for both interventions and PSHE and health education.

An example of how a school looks to provide support to pupils within a whole school approach is outlined below:

- All pupils able to access learning mentors and wellbeing project (universal provision)

- Health education (universal provision)

- Partnership with local training provider resulting in 40 trainee students offering counselling sessions via self and targeted referrals (getting help) – approaching local health trusts and universities can be very fruitful

- Pupils can also access art therapy (getting help)

- Nominated senior leadership team (SLT) member to manage onward referral to specialist services (getting more help).

CHAPTER 2

Bulging at the Seams

Exploring the Modern Policy Context for Mental Health and Drug Education and Prevention

This chapter will guide you in gaining increased understanding of the development of drug and alcohol education in order to help grasp some of the issues PSHE and health education leads face with the planning and delivery of this content. To do this we need to consider its position not only within a wider education context, but also within the wider discourse of drug use in society. In the absence of long-term effective approaches to mental health education specifically, the views the public hold of 'drugs' and 'drug addicts', and how these impact on both the individual and wider community, need to be considered in the development of drug and mental health education. This chapter will pay heed to this, not simply to provide a potted history of the topic, but rather to explore the inter-generational views of drugs and alcohol which influence the outlook of young people, teachers and other professionals working with young people today. This exploration will therefore give us a useful starting point for the delivery of drug and alcohol education within the modern school system. First, we will take a brief look at the development of PSHE as a subject and how its curriculum requirements and content as a non-statutory subject have changed dramatically alongside wider social and political concerns. Second, we will look at drug and alcohol education specifically and how attitudes and ideas on what effective delivery looks like have changed.

PSHE has had a chequered past in English schools and the English political system, with many of these factors being replicated throughout the rest of the UK. This past has been characterised by appreciation of the benefits of PSHE amongst health and to some extent education professionals, against varying degrees of resistance and support among the political establishment. It has enjoyed peaks and troughs in terms of this support, as well as its perceived relevance within an increasingly crowded National Curriculum. It is within this somewhat dysfunctional system that mental health and drug and alcohol education finds itself.

The benefits of an emotionally well and healthy child have been documented by key national bodies including Ofsted (2013) and the PSHE Association (2015). Government departments have also followed suit through the Department for Education (2014) and Public Health England (2015). While these benefits have been long espoused, there has never really been political consensus on whether PSHE should be a statutory subject with protected time within the National Curriculum. While this was tantalisingly close to coming to fruition in 2010, when the PSHE element of the Children's Schools and Families Bill essentially ran out of time before Parliament closed for the 2010 General Election, we currently have PSHE existing as a 'recommended' part of school life. The current wording within the National Curriculum reflects the government's slightly confusing view that while it isn't a statutory subject, there is still an expectation that it is covered:

> All schools should make provision for personal, social, health and economic education (PSHE), drawing on good practice. Schools are also free to include other subjects or topics of their choice in planning and designing their own programme of education. (National Curriculum, 2015)

This confusion is apparent in schools themselves, where staff often consider PSHE to be a statutory subject, or are at least of the strong opinion that it should be (PSHE Association, 2015). In part this has to be viewed as a positive legacy of the National Healthy Schools Programme which, alongside the Teenage Pregnancy Strategy of 1998, brought pupil health and wellbeing to the forefront of education as well as health policy. It displays a level of support and understanding of the benefits of PSHE which is furthered through the assertion that 88 per cent of teachers, 90 per cent of parents and 85 per cent of business leaders are in support of statutory status (PSHE Association, 2015).

It is also testament to those areas which still maintain roles supporting PSHE and Healthy Schools ethos in their local schools. Unfortunately, the slow death of a co-ordinated 'National' Healthy Schools Programme, central funding of the PSHE teacher training programme and the removal of the skills and family agendas from the DfE remit, has resulted in a gradual separation of education and health policy. So the strong bonds between both sectors have drifted and we are left with a vacuum in which PSHE currently sits, trying to be a jack of all trades but without the support to be a master of them. This is a generalization, of course, as we know where excellent PSHE is being delivered (Ofsted, 2013) as well as the links between outstanding PSHE and an outstanding school (PSHE Association 2015), even if there are limitations on determining causality within this relationship. However, the effectiveness of PSHE and drug and alcohol education within it will be severely limited while we still have wide variation in the quality and support for its delivery.

The good news is that recent developments are pointing towards a change in direction for PSHE within the National Curriculum. The DfE consultation of 2017–18 has resulted in a timetable for relationship and sex education (RSE) to become statutory within a wider programme of 'health education', by 2020. The exact wording and plans for supporting schools in achieving this are being consulted on at the time of writing, but the hope is for this to produce a more proactive, skills-based model of delivery rather than the reactive, knowledge-based models schools have been resigned to adopting.

A well-meaning but reactive system

We could trace the beginnings of the modern context for PSHE back to wider health concerns such as the harms caused by smoking, HIV and the rise of heroin and ecstasy use in the 1980s, through to perceived increases in under-age sex and teenage pregnancy in the 1990s, and the media-coined term of 'binge drinking' in the 2000s. Indeed, more recent additions to the PSHE roster (and safeguarding through regular updates to the UK government's Keeping Children Safe in Education guidance) include coverage of mental health, female genital mutilation (FGM), addressing children at risk of sexual exploitation (CSE), e-safety, domestic violence and the modern phenomenon of novel psychoactive substances (NPS) – otherwise known as 'legal highs' (these will be referred to as NPS from now on). It is under these overly reactive, ever-changing, ever-expanding expectations of a non-statutory subject, often without dedicated curriculum time, that drug and alcohol education in particular currently sits.

The development of PSHE along these topic-based lines has resulted in a tendency to deliver its content in segmented and discrete ways, using each *topic* to guide delivery. This is entirely understandable when a PSHE lead is tasked with creating a programme responding to these external pressures, and the media concern of the day. So we end up with delivery models based on some weeks delivering solely relationship and sex education, followed by some time on alcohol, then some time on e-safety, then if we are lucky we could squeeze in some sessions on mental health. It is against this backdrop that we can ask the question posed in the title of this chapter – is PSHE and health education 'bulging at the seams'?

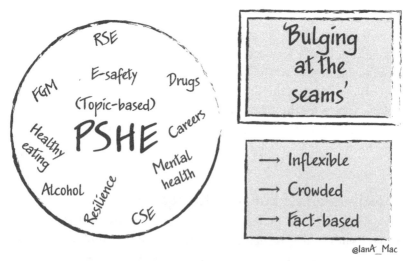

Figure 2.1: Current models of PSHE delivery

For many schools, the lack of statutory footing means dedicated curriculum time for drug education comes secondary to extra support sessions which have a more direct impact on pupil attainment. Again this is an understandable decision for some, given the performance measures school leaders adhere to around Maths and English targets, especially as these subjects now carry double weighting for the all-important Attainment 8 measures. It is this element which can further exacerbate the gap between education and health professionals. It does however hide a short-term approach which negates the links between a healthy, happy child being a well-achieving one (Public Health England, 2015). To help explore how schools currently deliver the topic, we will now look at three common models of delivery.

In many cases PSHE and wider health education can sometimes be delivered via the 'drop-day' approach, where pupils are taken off timetable for a day to receive intensive delivery on a given topic. This could be a day of drug education, mental health education, a combination of wider PSHE topics, or a part of other enrichment activities. This can often be championed by school leaders as an effective way of covering a topic, in spite of evidence and recommended practice being strongly against it as the *only* way of delivering PSHE. Previous Ofsted inspection criteria for PSHE highlighted that delivery solely by drop-days should be considered inadequate provision, and requiring improvement (2013). Limitations of this approach are also highlighted by Mentor-ADEPIS (2014), the Sex Education Forum (2018) and the PSHE Association itself. This approach is undoubtedly furthered through the non-statutory status of PSHE and health education, so it is hoped the new curriculum for 2020 will address this somewhat.

Adopting this approach can often have the unintended consequence of raising awareness about a given topic without allowing pupils the time to explore it fully and consolidate their learning. It can offer the opportunity for external specialists and local services to enrich delivery which has its own benefits, especially if pupils are gaining insight into their local young person's drug and alcohol service. From a pedagogical perspective this approach also has its limitations in whether content can be suited to the needs of the group, in addition to whether these visitors are sufficiently skilled and qualified to deliver that content in the first place. Toolkits are out there for schools to use to help with this process through bodies such as the PSHE Association, Mentor-ADEPIS and the Sex Education Forum, and it would be hoped that organisations offering services to schools are adhering to the DfE standards for school-based CPD (2016). However, this is also a time when funding for these external services is becoming tighter and their time more precious, so schools delivering the drop-day approach need to be considering its sustainability against these changes.

The dichotomy is that where the drop-day approach is maintained, pupil feedback will often be quoted as evidence in support of this approach. In later chapters we will look in more depth at evaluation and measuring impact, but for the time being it is sufficient to say this 'evidence' is a little shaky at best. This is particularly the case where process questions are asked such as 'did you enjoy the sessions today?' or 'did you learn something new about alcohol?' These questions are fine when combined with wider impact outcomes around changes in attitude or health behaviours, but if a pupil's baseline is no drug education at all then they are going to answer in positive terms as at least they are getting something! Moving away from this model of delivery as the sole opportunity for mental health and drug and alcohol education should therefore be considered a priority not only for schools and school leaders, but also for local public health teams for whom PSHE has a direct influence on health outcomes for the young people they serve. It is hoped that the move towards the statutory status for RSE within the wider scheme of health education from 2020 will support this shift towards evidence-based approaches.

Drug and alcohol education

The development of drug and alcohol education often refers to every drug worker's favourite 1980s example – Zammo from the children's television programme *Grange Hill*, and its associated Just Say No campaign. This covered the still extremely rare story of a schoolboy using heroin; however, for it to be so ingrained in the public consciousness we have to accept it has had a lasting influence. While the 'Just Say No' mantra has long been undermined as an effective drug education method, its meaning unfortunately has lasting currency across society. Responses in the tabloid media to drug-related incidents involving young people and drugs still hark back to 'tell them all the bad stuff and they won't do it'. Again, adopting this and other shock tactic approaches are lacking in evidence (Mentor-ADEPIS, 2017). After all, focusing on the rare but extreme risks often fails to gain credence with groups of young people who will know others using these substances who are coming to lower levels of harm. These approaches, therefore, immediately impact on the credibility given to educators and the education pupils receive. This pupil/educator relationship is something we will return to in a later chapter.

More recently, the government's Talk to Frank campaign has been promoted as the de facto information source on young people and drugs. Parliamentary questions on what the government has been spending to reduce the harm caused to young people by drugs and alcohol are referred to the Frank website and its associated media campaigns. Controversially, it could be argued that the allure of drugs as something 'deviant' and misunderstood by the older generation was in part furthered through some of the information campaigns run by Talk to Frank. This may seem like an over-reaction, but examples such as the 'Brain Warehouse' adverts, where a young cannabis user was presented as making a choice from a range of brains as a result of using the substance, only confused the issue while having limited impact on the audience it sought to influence (BBC News, 2013). The 'Brain Warehouse' campaign depicted a young person entering into a shop of brains, with the inference being that choosing to use cannabis meant choosing a different brain. While it may have been correct to make a link between cannabis use and mental health, there was no mention of what impacts on this risk, including amount of use, strength of cannabis, pre-existing conditions or other factors in an individual's life which can make mental ill health more likely. Without these extra elements of context, young people found the campaign confusing and in some cases misleading. However, this all sits comfortably within the so called 'war on drugs' which has placed any substance covered by the Misuse of Drugs Act as the choice of deviants, 'yobs' and those generally too weak to say no. This is not the place for in-depth discussion of the validity of the war on drugs, but it certainly makes for an invigorating classroom debate at Key Stage 4 (Mentor-ADEPIS, 2017).

Understanding the source of these viewpoints on drugs and drug users is important when devising programmes of drug education. Some pupils will already hold such views, often as a result of parental influence and education at home. Some pupils will come from families where drug use is the 'norm' for them, and so they are likely to be more sensitive to the 'demon drug user' stereotype. Others may already have developed a more nuanced view, understanding that drug use is something impacted by many influences including the media, social circumstance, parental drug use, and the social connections we all make. Ensuring a drug education programme is based on evidence and accurate information is therefore essential in order to challenge misperceptions, while enabling them to assess risks associated with drugs and alcohol appropriately.

Where wider society is still promoting the evidence-lacking approaches discussed earlier as effective responses to drug issues and drug-related incidents in schools, this causes problems for PSHE leads. Recent discourse around NPS gives a good example, where schools were coming under pressure from the outside to be tackling the issue – even 'fixing' it. This is exemplified by increases in requests for NPS-related materials. This pressure naturally fed into the classic treatment of PSHE by delivering specific topic-based information to pupils. NPS shows the limitations of this approach for two key reasons. First, the changing nature of the NPS market meant that substances were continually being altered to keep one step ahead of legislative powers to make them illegal. This subsequently meant that as soon as a resource was made available to address a specific substance it would almost immediately be out of date. So addressing NPS in this reactive way is fraught with issues. Chapter 7 covers these issues in more detail, including possible approaches to adopt within drug and alcohol education.

Second, it undermines the proactive potential of PSHE and health education – something which PSHE leads are becoming almost conditioned into negating. In this I am referring to the life skills developed through the subject which become applicable across its topic areas. This idea of life skills is one which will be referred to consistently throughout the rest of this book. The PSHE Association has rightly sought to address this with their recent Programme of Study for PSHE (2018) through the suggested reorganising of the subject into three skill-based areas:

- Health and wellbeing

- Relationships

- Living in the wider world.

Adopting a 'life skills' approach to drug and alcohol education is something we will return to in subsequent chapters, and has been promoted by a range of organisations as a more effective approach to drug education (Mentor ADEPIS, 2017; Public Health England,

2015). It is also something local public health teams need to play a greater role in promoting, in light of the applicability of these skills in addressing wider risk-taking behaviours of young people. The image in Figure 2.2 shows a starting point for thinking about how this change in approach can open up PSHE to being more responsive to pupil needs at individual schools.

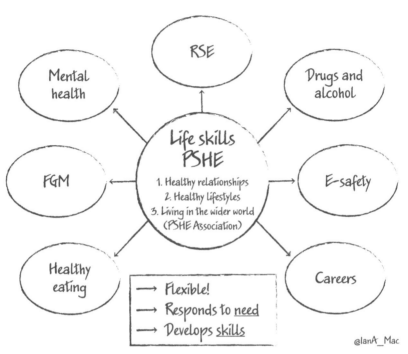

Figure 2.2: Life skills approaches to PSHE

Mental health education

In a very similar way to drug and alcohol education, mental health education in schools can currently take many forms and be subject to a range of descriptions, some of which are not totally helpful. This is in part because of the generalised way in which we talk about the promotion of positive mental health, and the prevention of mental ill health. As a catch-all term we often hear the phrase 'mental health awareness'. It is a term I have come to struggle with, as for some it can mean everything we want it to – promoting positive mental health and wellbeing, providing the opportunity to practise healthy coping and asking for help when needed, while also identifying when we don't feel great and how to respond to that. However, it can also mean a very simplistic understanding of 'mental health' – just facts about what certain mental health conditions are, without any content aimed at upskilling young people or changing their attitudes towards their own and others' mental health. It is these latter elements which are most important within mental health education, yet it is those which are often missed for the reasons outlined earlier. I have heard of young people being quite traumatised by being shown a television documentary on mental health in the interests of 'raising awareness'. This being done in isolation and not as part of a wider programme of health education resulted in it being a distressing experience. In this way, mental health education can be subject to the 'something is better than nothing' approach described earlier, and not one which is delivered in a safe and effective way. It is the unintentional harm caused by these approaches which the new 2020 curriculum on health education should seek to address.

There are some effective tools out there which schools can access – Time to Change, Young Minds and the PSHE Association all have accessible tools and resources – although ensuring that any content derived from elsewhere meets the needs of the pupils in front of you is really important. Especially when these resources are of very good quality, it is easy to fall into the trap of 'delivering to the resource'. This means effectively reproducing the sessions verbatim, without first checking whether it is pitched at the right level, fits in within a school's wider programme of health education, or meets any specific needs of the class or year group being delivered to. This harks back to the importance of pupil voice and curriculum in the whole school approach, and can just prompt us to question the validity of the chosen resources. In many cases these tools will be relevant and of value to your school, but we just need to promote the process of quality assuring these tools and their functions ourselves.

Transforming support for those who need it

Asking what can be done to best support the mental health needs of children and young people generally results in a common theme to responses – funding. Local CAMHS teams often bear the brunt of criticism from universal services about long waiting lists, high thresholds for assessments and general despair from those frontline staff in education and social care making referrals. This has contributed to an estimation that only 25–35 per cent of those with a diagnosable mental health condition were accessing support (Department of Health, 2015). In a similar way to changing how we think about PSHE delivery, in many ways it is too simplistic to assume increasing funding will fix the system – another reactive way of approaching the issue.

In 2015 the Department of Health released its 'Future in Mind' strategy document (Department of Health, 2015) which outlined plans for transforming how children and young people's mental health and wellbeing are supported. The key themes to this process were outlined as:

1. Promoting resilience, prevention and early intervention

2. Improving access to effective support – a system without tiers

3. Care for the most vulnerable

4. Accountability and transparency

5. Developing the workforce. (Department of Health, 2015)

As part of this process, every Clinical Commissioning Group (CCGs – the collective of local GPs who make decisions on how health services are funded locally) in England was tasked with producing its own Local Transformation Plan (LTP) outlining how the recommendations from Future in Mind were to be put into practice. These should be widely available in each area, so a quick internet search should offer this up for you. Schools and the education system were identified as a key stakeholder at these local levels and were strongly encouraged to take part in this process. Regardless of this recommendation and whether schools were widely consulted in local areas, my own personal experience of working with and supporting those frontline staff in schools who work with those pupils in need and making referrals, was that they had never come across these plans – either locally or nationally.

To fully appreciate the context for the current Local Transformation Plans, we do need to briefly consider how those very same services have developed over time and contributed to the current state of the CAMHS system. At the root of CAMHS as we know it coming into existence was an adoption of adult models of delivery for a young people's service. An understandable decision at the time, I'm sure, but ultimately one which fails to take into account the fact that young people access services in very different ways from adults. At the core of this model are the dreaded 'tiers' of delivery. Pastoral teams I have worked with over the years would probably consider 'tears' to be a better spelling of that model, given the struggles they would often describe in accessing support for their pupils. Commissioning services along those lines may have simplified the system for adult services, but within young people services it only created an inflexible model which made it hard for services to respond effectively to the needs of young people being referred.

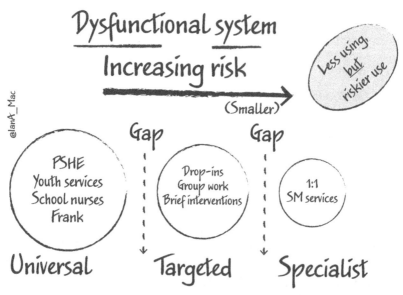

*SM= substance misuse

Figure 2.3: Traditional models of children and young people mental health support

School staff and other frontline professionals find themselves at the universal level of this model (effectively Tier 1) and responding to both early signs of distress and deteriorating health among pupils, as well as crises. At this stage we should add that the model assumes that information at the universal level should be enough for most people to manage their health behaviours effectively – those who are unable to are the ones needing further support up the tiers. Yet, if that information is being delivered at that universal level through non-statutory models of PSHE by unsupported and untrained staff, then that is always likely to result in increased numbers needing support further up the system. It also assumes that those staff may be aware of their role within this system, whereas anecdotally some school staff report being unaware of their role within any wider system of support:

> Schools are not aware of the tiers of delivery – I am only learning of this recently. Another example of the two worlds of education and health not meeting. (Secondary SLT member in conversation with author)

This quote is all the more alarming as Future in Mind has ensured we are moving to a newer tierless model of delivery in England, suggesting there is a lot of work to do in engaging schools and school staff in how young people's mental health is supported in the community. With this in mind, who else provides support at that universal level? First, we can consider the important role of youth workers, especially for those young people who may struggle in traditional educational settings. However, youth services have seen unprecedented cuts in service and a general lack of national strategy (Local Government Association, 2017). We can also consider school nursing teams who themselves have experienced decreases in funding and increased responsibility around safeguarding and the statutory delivery of national programmes such as the National Child Measurement Programme, and national screening and vaccination programmes. While this has impacted on their capacity to support health education in schools and the need to keep up to date with the evidence base, this professional group is moving back towards more focused delivery activity.

When all these factors are considered alongside decreased funding to universal public health services at local levels, the wider impacts of austerity and poor determinants of health, it is unsurprising we have seen increased need for support over the last ten years – support which the tiered model of delivery has been unable to contend with. The expectation for pupils and their families to travel, in some cases long distances, to appointments should be viewed as a legacy of adopting adult models of delivery. However, this is ultimately a state of affairs which those most in need of support were unable to contend with.

We know young people struggle to access services in adolescence anyway (the dropping of the 'You're Welcome' programme which aimed to address access to services still fills me with great disappointment), so expecting them to travel to unknown areas only adds to this, while creating a big gap between tiers of service for them to fall through. The consequence of this? The creation of a funnel of need which local services could not ever address, increased thresholds to maintain some level of service to those who need it most, and ultimately an 'all or nothing' response once that threshold was reached. It's no wonder CAMHS services found themselves between a rock and a hard place.

So it is against this backdrop that Future in Mind has sought to transform the CAMHS service model. As well as specific improvements in eating disorders services where specific need has been identified, LTPs are focused on closing the gaps in provision the tiered model has unintentionally produced, focusing on the key themes of Future in Mind outlined above. Closing these gaps will look to reduce the number of young people falling through those gaps and requiring intensive support by providing that support earlier.

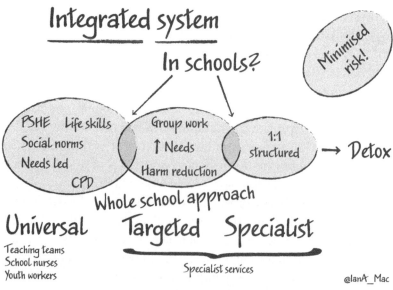

Figure 2.4: Closing the gaps

Ultimately though it is about changing mindsets across the whole system and producing a model where the system fits around young people rather than expecting young people to fit around the system. This means them accessing services where they feel most comfortable and safe. In the main, this means schools. This should, however, mean schools as the buildings rather than the staff within them. So it isn't about pastoral and other school staff delivering that support, just them facilitating other services to access those young people and families in timely ways. It is true though that some young people will not want or need that support to be delivered by a specialist team and therefore will benefit most from universal staff offering some support. Strategies for this are discussed in more detail in Chapter 9. But for those who do need onward referral, we should hope this means a stepped approach to support rather than the 'all or nothing' one we have got used to, and ultimately one with young people leading and being involved in their own support and care. That said, it has to be about improved outcomes across the board, which is something we can *all* contribute to.

When applying learning from all this into practice, we therefore need to consider the wider system and influences in which mental health and drug and alcohol education issues are placed – in terms of their historical development, how young people view them, and how the adults around them view them too. We have concentrated more on the historical influences here, and highlighted how we have been conditioned into the 'Just Say No' approach, and the wider view of drug use being something which is 'other' and detached from reality. We need to be aware of these influences when communicating the benefits of a well-planned drug education programme to parents, governors and the wider community. At times this can include explaining why these shock tactics are not effective and are without an evidence base.

Things to remember:

- The links between improved wellbeing of pupils and staff and academic attainment are well documented (Public Health England, 2015).

- Previous approaches to drug education focusing on 'shock tactics' are not considered best practice (Mentor-ADEPIS, 2017).

- Mental health 'awareness' campaigns are not effective educational tools in themselves – they need to be supported with the development of key life skills and positive coping strategies.

- The use of off-curriculum drop-days in isolation to deliver PSHE can be counterproductive and is therefore considered 'not good enough' (Ofsted, 2013; PSHE Association, 2015; Public Health England, 2015). They should only be used to enhance the PSHE and health education provision already being delivered.

- Models of service delivery are being transformed to respond to the needs of pupils who need more effective support (Department of Health, 2015).

POINTS FOR PRACTICE

Sam Beal is the Partnership Adviser for Health and Wellbeing at Brighton and Hove City Council, and works with schools, public health and other relevant national and local services to improve whole school approaches to PSHE education. Sam outlines the strengths and challenges of the Brighton and Hove approach:

- A survey of pupil health behaviours that takes place every two years helps schools identify any trends or gaps in provision to focus on. This also helps monitor progress of any interventions as it gives a natural baseline of specific behaviours to measure impact against. Additionally, it provides data to ensure normative approaches are taken to the delivery of PSHE education.

- The presence of a PSHE network where local leads come together termly to share good practice, resources and access CPD around the subject has been very useful. Not only does this create a local community of practice, it also helps with establishing effective working partnerships across schools, and offers a place for peer support to take place.

- Maintaining consistent models of delivery can be very difficult, with schools sometimes moving from the desired model of dedicated curriculum time to less effective models of tutor time or even drop-days. This is understandable given the wider pressures school leadership teams find themselves under, although school-level pupil needs identified through the local pupil survey can help in maintaining as much curriculum time as possible.

— Accessing effective staff training is a constant barrier to any meaningful delivery of PSHE. This is rooted in lack of direct funds available, lack of time when competing with other CPD needs, and also schools knowing where to go for any CPD which follows best practice. In Brighton and Hove, schools have benefited from area-wide training events to cut down on cost, support from the local public health team, and signposting to online webinars from reputable sources.

— Schools have also agreed to an area-wide approach when it comes to topics to focus on around resources and CPD. This has helped protect against knee jerk responses, while also supporting longer-term planning around skills-based content which can underpin many topics within PSHE such as mental health, drugs and alcohol and RSE.

Brighton and Hove's PSHE network can be found on Twitter @PSHEedBH.

CHAPTER 3

Theoretical Models of Adolescent Health Behaviours and Support

We make day-to-day choices around our health choices and behaviours almost without thinking about it. These often unconscious decisions are influenced by a wide range of factors with an even wider range of possible consequences. A greater understanding of these factors can help us both manage our own health and wellbeing, as well as support those around us – whether that be pupils, colleagues or family. This chapter seeks to make sense of this in relation to young people of secondary school age, where factors around brain development, risk taking and identity formation are also of importance. This chapter will also look to explore these models and how other life events can influence health, including attachment theories, adverse childhood experiences (ACE) and wider risk-taking behaviours.

Social determinants

The work of Sir Michael Marmot (2010) has influenced the policy and practice of preventing ill health over the past ten years. It has specifically helped us look at the environments in which people live, work and experience the world around them, and how they influence health outcomes at both individual and community levels. These are more commonly termed the social determinants of health (The Marmot Review, 2010). What the report advocated was a much broader appreciation of how we can influence the lives and health of our communities by looking at society as a whole. This includes key things like housing, employment, access to health care, leisure time and leisure amenities, education and disability among others.

The Local Government Association (2018) has summarised negative impacts of these key social determinants of health as contributing to:

- People living in the poorest neighbourhoods in England will on average die seven years earlier than people living in the richest neighbourhoods.

- People living in poorer areas not only die sooner, but spend more of their lives with disability – an average total difference of 17 years.

- The Review highlights the social gradient of health inequalities – put simply, the lower one's social and economic status, the poorer one's health is likely to be.

- Health inequalities arise from a complex interaction of many factors – housing, income, education, social isolation, disability – all of which are strongly affected by one's economic and social status.

- It is estimated that the annual cost of health inequalities is between £36 billion and £40 billion through lost taxes, welfare payments and costs to the NHS.

- Action on health inequalities requires action across all the social determinants of health, including education, occupation, income, home and community.

It is this social background in which young people are growing up today, and taking note of this is essential if we are to support them to live happy and healthy lives. This also means that schools are not the only places for this learning to occur, although we do need to recognise the essential role schools play in this process – both as places to learn, but also as places where children and young people feel safe and secure. With this in mind, wider support needs to be offered around how we think about PSHE and health education, aligning the messages given by other universal professionals more closely with those within a programme of health education at school. Undoubtedly, there are inconsistencies in this in some areas up and down the country. Health and education professionals do come at the issue of pupil wellbeing from different perspectives as a result of very different training, different job roles, and working to different standards and practices. In the past there have been those within each local authority who supported that link between the two, often under the umbrella of the National Healthy Schools Programme. As has been discussed earlier, the gradual loss of these services and individuals and the changing nature of the school nursing role has meant the gap between education and health is larger than it has been. This has also been massively influenced by changes in both health and education policy and funding over that same time. However, in areas where those two professions have been bridged effectively, there has been strategic recognition of the need for education and public health to work more closely, as well as consistency of personnel.

It also needs to be recognised that as well as supporting schools around planning and training needs, some services are being commissioned to directly deliver PSHE and health education content to pupils in local schools. It is essential that these professional groups and services are also aware of what evidence-informed best practice looks like, and how this can be very different from what works in adult services. Without that, there is a risk of schools being expected to take one approach from an education perspective, and local health professionals expecting to deliver something different. My own experience of working within these local arrangements suggests that health commissioning of universal delivery can be quite patchy in terms of best practice. This is particularly the case when local services are commissioned to deliver according to the number of sessions delivered rather than ensuring evidence-based practice. This can mean reneging to a 'something is better than nothing' approach and therefore undermining good practice delivery which may be done in other local schools. This can be the case whether delivery is commissioned to a specific service or as part of a smaller pot of money to other community groups who may not necessarily be aware of specific needs within a given school or group of schools.

Social determinants of adolescent health

We know that in many cases, negative health outcomes for adolescents are also linked with social status and influenced by these social determinants of health. We know there are correlations between areas of deprivation and outcomes such as teen pregnancy rates, smoking rates in under 15s, and rates of childhood obesity. However, the rates of low self-esteem and self-harm among those young people living in less deprived areas suggest the factors influencing adolescent health are ever changing and evolving. To fully understand this, we also need to take into account the social and neurodevelopmental changes which are particularly important to young people today.

For the purposes of this chapter, a simplified look at brain development in adolescence can be adopted. With this in mind, we need to be aware of how the adolescent brain develops and grows over time. This process is still rooted in the prehistoric nature of human survival – in particular the 'fight or flight' response, which outlines how we are predisposed to respond to threats either by confronting them (fight) or by avoiding them (flight). This response has been essential to human survival and as such the area of the brain governing this response is the first to develop. Indeed, looking at pupil behaviour through this lens may help us gain a wider understanding of what those 'fight or flight' responses in the classroom may look like. Either way, a consequence of this is a very emotional way of responding to social situations, often by displaying negative behaviours. We have come to label some of these behaviours as toddler tantrums or teenage rebellion.

Part of the human condition – what it is that makes us 'human' – is developing the ability to control these responses. This section of the brain is what develops later in adolescence and helps us to make more logical decisions, despite experiencing what may be an initial emotional, 'fight or flight' response. Making these neural connections to support logical and reasoned decision making takes extensive practice, with many of us not having fully developed neural pathways until we have left 'adolescence' long behind us. So, young people are therefore hardwired to make decisions not in logical, well thought-out ways, but rather in impulsive ways with short-term benefits in mind. For many, these short-term benefits will be social in their nature – gaining kudos with their friends, finding a 'place' within a peer group, gaining appreciation and gratification from displaying a certain behaviour. It is worth reflecting whether drug education, mental health and wider health education planning takes these realities into account (this is explored in more detail in later chapters).

Attachment and trauma

Aligned with adolescent brain development is the concept of 'attachment'. This theory of attachment builds on the work of John Bowlby and at its root is the notion that from birth we strive to build and maintain deep emotional bonds with others, resulting in 'lasting psychological connectedness between human beings' (Bowlby, 1969, p.194). The most obvious example of this, and one which Bowlby and colleagues observed intently, is that between a newborn child and their mother. The parental role as care giver is essential in this process, and the separation of child from parent can be a source of great distress – something many parents or grandparents can relate to. Ultimately, the early years are a key stage for these attachments to be made, with Bowlby suggesting that if no secure attachments are made in this period then the child is likely to experience developmental difficulties and issues with regulating emotions. On the contrary, children who have been able to make secure attachments to others are likely to display 'self-understanding and insight, empathy for others and appropriate moral reasoning' (Rose, 2015). Developing these skills is a precursor for 'executive functions' which include problem solving, managing those impulsive 'fight or flight' responses referred to earlier, and the ability to make effective reasoned decisions. It is therefore important to consider the individual social histories of children when exploring certain behaviours they may be displaying, and even more important to look 'beyond the behaviour' to fully support and manage a young person's needs. More importantly this can also help us understand the deteriorating mental health of some young people, and the adoption of negative coping mechanisms. Indeed, there are regular calls for greater understanding of attachment within the wider school workforce (Shmueli-Goetz, 2018).

It is a lack of this attachment and executive functioning which can result in poor mental health and adoption of unhealthy coping mechanisms such as self-harm, drug and alcohol use and wider risky behaviours. It is suggested by some that this is also what can be influencing the increased importance of 'gang' cultures in adolescence. Indeed, the recent phenomenon of 'county lines' can also have links to vulnerable young people in this way. (This is a practice where young people from one area of the country are used in other areas to transport and deliver drugs instead of dealers. It is of personal interest how this practice has been going on for a number of years, but now it has its own terminology, it is finally receiving more focused policy responses.) From the perspective of adopting a whole school approach, greater appreciation of the impact of trauma is not only needed within the pastoral teams dealing with those pupils exhibiting such behaviours, but also within health education planning in terms of developing the skills in young people to adopt positive behaviours. As such, the development of a life skills approach (Mentor-ADEPIS, 2017; Public Health England, 2015; PSHE Association, 2018) to health education gains even more traction. The penultimate chapter of this book explores this in more detail. It is also of importance to stress that schools should not be seen as, nor see themselves as, the only ones who are involved in addressing these needs – rather they are a key part of the puzzle which should involve wider services and family input. Some of the historical issues outlined in Chapters 1 and 2 make this difficult, but they are also issues we need to overcome if the needs of pupils are to be truly put at the centre of any support offered to them as required by Future in Mind.

What attachment issues also bring to mind is the importance of transition from Key Stage 2 to Key Stage 3 – not just in terms of familiarisation and desensitising of pupils to the workings of secondary school, but more importantly in terms of how attachments may be formed in a very different environment from primary school. Let us not forget that in the UK, the primary school system is very much one of nurture, based on the strong relationships built between pupils and teacher which are formed by consistent and repeated day-to-day interactions in a relatively closed and controlled environment. Even where some class teaching may be done on a job share basis, pupils still spend upwards of two days a week intensively with the same teaching staff. While this relationship is understandably different from the parent/child one mentioned earlier, the nature and level of interaction is likely to bring with it its own certain levels of 'attachment'. Children are therefore accustomed to developing their pupil/teacher relationships in this very linear way each year. It roots them in the classroom as a safe place, and one with static and stable relationships – with the adults, fellow pupils and learning environment in which they find themselves. Indeed, models of resilience acknowledge the importance of a 'secure base' in developing the ability of children to cope with life's ups and downs, as shown in Figure 3.1 (Daniel and Wassell, 2002).

Figure 3.1: A model of resilience
Source: adapted from Daniel and Wassell (2002)

The disruption of this relationship after transition to secondary education, and its impact on the wellbeing of pupils, is therefore something which needs greater attention. The very nature of secondary education, with its multiple and discrete subjects with new teachers to get used to, makes the forming of attachments and a secure base a more daunting prospect. Yes, pupils have nominated tutors to support their pastoral care, but one short session a week means this relationship is again likely to be very different from that in primary education. Now those pupils who have had a secure base and secure attachments since early childhood are likely to have developed some level of executive functioning to manage this transition. For those pupils who haven't, this transition becomes all the more difficult, distressing and likely to impact negatively on mental health. I have visited many schools that pride themselves on strong health education and a nurturing ethos throughout all members of the school community. This includes making pupils aware of where they can access support around their health and wellbeing, and who can support them. On the face of it this would be considered good practice and something to be applauded. However, when these pupils have been asked whether they would actually access that support in a range of scenarios, they have tended to err on the side of caution and when asked about accessing support 'for a friend' in school they respond with a resounding 'NO WAY!'

These considerations are particularly prevalent in Key Stage 3 pupils who may still be looking for those attachments to fully grasp school as a safe place. It also highlights the distinction there is to be made between making pupils aware of where they can access support and them actually being able to access it. This is the difference between knowing where to go, and actually having the ability and capacity to access it. The ability to actually knock on that door and walk through that threshold. To actually have the skills to open up and tell their story, and the confidence in that staff member to do the right thing and not just go straight to social services. In many schools, regardless of status, the 'where' is something that is done quite well – the 'how' is what needs work. I have delivered workshops in schools with excellent PSHE which is delivered to current best practice, yet when presented with a practical real-life scenario of supporting a friend to access help, school is still seen as somewhere pupils view with suspicion. They know who in school they can approach, and where they need to go, yet there are still barriers to them accessing that support. In those examples, pupils will often talk about the extreme consequences – normally around social services being involved and them being removed. Of course this is not what schools are saying in their safeguarding policies, yet we need to acknowledge that some pupils still have this view. Giving practical examples of support being offered in a safe and realistic way can help challenge these perceptions, along with practical role play of pupils asking for help. This helps them develop a language of support and breaks down those barriers. This process is particularly important when we look at the recommendations from the Future in Mind report and recent Local Transformation Plans, where 'school' is highlighted as being an important place for young people to access early intervention around mental health support. A fantastic colleague of mine from the

Charlie Waller Memorial Trust, Rachel Welch, has coined the term 'the 3Ps' for schools to strive for when promoting access to services and support – safe people, safe policies and safe places. Where all these are in place, we can be sure a school is working in the right direction.

Closely linked to issues around attachment is the impact on children who have experienced trauma in their lives, or adverse childhood experiences (ACEs). This trauma can be experienced in many ways, whether through bereavement, abuse, neglect or exposure to one or more of the 'toxic trio' – domestic abuse, parental substance use or parental mental illness. Similarly to the impact of a lack of attachment, we know the presence of ACEs in a child's history can impact on brain development and those higher functions, thus impacting on their mental health and their behavioural responses to stress-inducing situations. While both can be present in a child's history, we do need to be careful not to use these terms interchangeably. Additionally, we need to recognise that ACEs may represent a set of complex and individualised experiences a child will have gone through, and they cannot be solved or healed with a simple 'intervention'. Whole school approaches which include the support of wider services to help pupils to develop their own skills and strategies, to explore and develop positive language around their emotions, and identify not just where to access support but *how* to, are all key elements to consider – not just a screening process or mindfulness intervention in isolation. Indeed, the current trend of screening children and young people for things like ACEs or substance use also needs to be treated with caution. While these tools may seem useful in identifying those pupils who may need extra support, that support has to be in place before any screening takes place. These practices can also take away the individual nature of a young person's experiences, with focus being drawn to whether a score falls into a certain range. This represents a further point for collaboration for schools and wider services around ensuring interventions are available and suitable for those who need it.

Resilience

The concept of resilience is one which has in recent years become increasingly common when referring to helping young people develop socially and psychologically. It is commonly referenced as something young people need to 'have' in order to be successful and thrive during adolescence, and therefore something those who work with young people should seek to develop in them. Indeed, the Department for Education's vision for health education post 2020 is for it to 'support the development of qualities such as confidence, resilience, self respect and self control', and that it teaches pupils 'how to build mental resilience and wellbeing'. For such a central concept to policy and practice within education, health and wider universal services for children and young people, there is little in these policy statements around what 'resilience' actually *is*. Without clear definitions in place, I have been in many schools where staff are aware of the need to build resilience in their pupils (let alone themselves), yet have not had the opportunity to fully explore what that actually means in practice. The result is an understandable lack of consensus over what they are actually trying to achieve. If we are not working towards an agreed definition and set of parameters around 'resilience' then the risk is that people are pulling in slightly different directions. This is where we need that more concrete understanding of what we mean by 'resilience', and how do we know if pupils actually have it?

The Boing Boing collective at the University of Brighton have a very interesting chronology of how resilience has been and continues to be defined, incorporating elements around the ideas of bouncing back, overcoming odds, coping with adversity. Ultimately I agree with Hart *et al.*'s (2016) definition, who put it as:

> Overcoming adversity, whilst also potentially changing, or even dramatically transforming, aspects of that adversity. (p.3)

For me it is the changing of the aspects of adversity that is key. If we take the 'bouncing back' analogy, that is something likened to a bouncy ball which will bounce back into the hands after it is dropped. However, if we drop that ball and rather than catch it when it returns to the top of the bounce, we let it continue to bounce, what happens? The ball starts to lose height with every bounce, not quite bouncing back as high as it did before, until it frantically tries to keep bouncing just before it stops doing so at all. I use this a lot to describe the limitations with just assuming that resilience is about the ability to 'bounce back'. Being able to bounce back once doesn't necessarily mean we are able to keep doing that each time we hit adversity.

Figure 3.2: Is resilience about more than 'bouncing back'?

Figure 3.3: Changing the aspects of adversity

Instead of simply bouncing back, and to use Hart *et al*.'s (2016) idea of changing aspects of that adversity, can we look to change the conditions in which that ball is bouncing to keep it bouncing? We can gently tap it at the top of each bounce – not hitting it though as that would make us lose control of it. We can lift it after a couple of bounces so it returns to the starting point. Or we can change the surface on which it is bouncing. All these things can serve to keep that ball bouncing back, and effectively are a bit of a toolkit for how that ball can keep doing so. So if we translate that analogy back to the lives of young people and a working definition of resilience, we can explore how to change those aspects of adversity which Hart refers to. It is really important we understand this doesn't mean referring pupils into large interventions or specific programmes. At a universal level, it refers to simple things we can do in the context of our own job roles to create what Ann Masten terms 'ordinary magic' (cited in Hart *et al.*, 2016). These are actions which may seem small and perhaps of little significance to the professional, but to the person lacking resilience, they can have large impacts. This is where we can use Daniel and Wassell's (2002) model of resilience to help think about putting this into practice (see Figure 3.1).

Each domain in this model represents an element which ordinary magic can impact on, and if we can grow one or more of the bubbles then we can contribute to changing the aspect of adversity an individual is facing, and therefore contribute to their resilience. To take each one in turn:

- *Secure base* – for some pupils this will be home, or for others this could be school itself. For the latter, we can assume that Friday afternoons are likely to be a difficult time for these pupils as they may see the weekend as being a time without that secure and safe base. So checking in with these pupils at these times can help reinforce school as a secure and safe place for them, and that it will still be there on Monday morning. It also means that a clear and individualised welcome into school on a Monday morning can help them settle back into a secure routine.

- *Social competence* – this is something which in many ways is at the core of effective life skills based PSHE and health education. It reflects the skills young people develop both inside and outside of school which demonstrate an ability to act, behave and interact in changing social circumstances. This could be through voluntary activities, supporting school open evenings, or acting as a mentor for younger pupils. Even small acts of kindness and thoughtfulness can be reinforced as showing a level of social competence and therefore contributing to the development of resilience.

- *Talents and interests* – we can often think about this in terms of gifted and talented programmes within education, but taking a more individualised approach to this can reap benefits. Finding ways to highlight or reinforce those talents a pupil has, however small, can help them change how they view that skill and acknowledge its role in making them who they are. Again, ordinary magic suggests this doesn't need to be a big gesture at an assembly (for some pupils that would be counterproductive) but could just be acknowledging that in the corridor or dinner queue.

- *Positive values* – this has some links with social competence and again is supported by effective PSHE and health education. This can be about the values a school promotes as part of its mission statement around acceptance, promoting diversity, and respecting the views of others.

- *Friendships* – in many ways this needs to be more about *positive* friendships, and helping pupils identify not only what contributes to a good and supportive friendship, but also putting that into practice. As is explored elsewhere, that can be difficult when young people are searching for their own identity and acceptance amongst their peers. So the more we can promote principles of good friendships, the more we can contribute to developing effective resilience.

- *Education* – we should really take this in its widest sense, and it is something which can easily become all encompassing as a form of 'academic resilience'. While attainment is a part of defining success and development in school years, acknowledging the small steps some pupils take along their own educational journeys is key in reinforcing their ability to make achievements despite some adversities. These could be long-standing social circumstances, or they could be more transient ones such as illness, changes in teachers, family bereavements, etc.

POINTS FOR PRACTICE

When it comes to schools ensuring they are supporting pupils to build resilience, Lucas Shelemy and Pooky Knightsmith (2017) have drawn out the idea of '4Ps' from an extensive review of the literature on building resilience and addressing adversity in children and young people:

- *Parents* – the role of early attachment is a key factor highlighted by the evidence base, and the role of a trusted teacher or other adult in school can help boost resilience in vulnerable young people.

- *Peers* – this recognises positive peer relationships where the young person feels a sense of belonging and acceptance, identifies with a group of like-minded peers, feels supported and respected, and puts more emphasis on a few high-quality friendships rather than many superficial ones.

- *Problem solving* – this acknowledges the link between the ability to think through problems and offer workable solutions, with increased coping skills. A timetabled health curriculum is an essential factor in schools teaching these skills and allowing young people to practise them.

- *Passion* – this highlights the role of having 'something' a young person feels a passion towards in building resilience and coping. This can be a hobby or other interest, and participation in these has been shown to divert attention away from negative experiences, while also boosting confidence, problem solving and self-efficacy. (Adapted from Shelemy and Knightsmith, 2017)

Pooky can be found on Twitter @PookyH.

CHAPTER 4

Alcohol, Smoking, Social Norms and Engaging Parents

Traditional perceptions around young people's alcohol use have arguably been informed by mediated views of the deviant youth and the binge drinking phenomenon. Do these perceptions and media representations hold up to scrutiny, and ultimately how do they influence young people's behaviour choices? Depending on editorial stance, newspaper stories on youth alcohol use are often imbued with a sense of moral panic or notions of a feral youth, or an inevitable product of social circumstance – the truth is probably somewhere in between. These news stories are regularly supported by the stock image of 'drunk girl on street bench'. You will have seen it – young-looking female in black dress slumped over street bench with bottle of alcohol nearby. Regardless of whether said news story is negative (the deviant, feral youth one) or positive, the stock image is often rolled out. This chapter will explore trends in use and perceptions of alcohol and smoking among young people, and the concept of social norms in a whole school approach to alcohol use.

Alcohol

The general trend for the number of 11–15-year-olds who have ever had an alcoholic drink (defined as a whole one, not just a sip) is encouraging. It has steadily dropped from 62 per cent in 1990 to 38 per cent by 2014. This figure is the one often quoted when there are positive stories around the issue. Whether this drop is a result of improved alcohol education, or reduced availability, is open to debate.

As with many universal public health interventions, controlling for specific factors in analysing these phenomena is extremely difficult. Either way, the usefulness of data on the numbers who have *tried* alcohol needs to be questioned in my view. Of more relevance for PSHE and health education planning is data around continued and habitual behaviours – in this case the numbers of young people who are drinking weekly, and how much those who do drink are drinking. Again, data shows the numbers drinking in the last week has dropped from 25 per cent in 2003 to only 8 per cent in 2014. However, the mean unit consumption has fluctuated over that period. This data shows the devil is in the detail, suggesting that while the numbers of young people who are drinking is declining, those who are drinking alcohol may be drinking more.

What is behind this data? Again, proving causation is difficult but we can make educated guesses based on correlations and what we do know from experiential evidence, for instance, for areas with high levels of young people drinking weekly, with the numbers of young people who say they get their alcohol from home. In some cases, this is without parental knowledge, but more frequently it is given to them *by* parents. Now this isn't about bashing parental influence here (!), simply identifying a key link highlighted by data. Likely behind this is the idea of the continental approach to alcohol in adolescence – namely 'if you give it to them early they will learn to respect it'. This negates recommendations from the Chief Medical Officer for England that children should remain alcohol free before age 15. It also negates evidence showing for every year under 15 young people are exposed to alcohol use they are 10 per cent more likely to come to alcohol-related harm in later life.

Coping mechanisms

In many ways we need to view alcohol use in a similar way to other negative coping mechanisms for young people's mental health. This includes self-harm behaviour, risky sexual behaviour, violent outbursts, etc. Professionals acknowledge the reasons for a young person drinking alcohol may be very similar to the reasons they (and adults) may exercise, play video games or even drink coffee.

Data sources around youth behaviours are commonly scrutinised for their usefulness. Those who subscribe to the deviant youth perspective are likely to minimise the relevance of this data, questioning whether young people will respond truthfully. However, in many areas local surveys and data collection methods correlate with the larger national datasets (Brighton and Hove, Derbyshire) and help add greater weight to the results. We can also debunk the idea that asking pupils about their alcohol and drug use makes them more likely to try these substances by raising the awareness of them. Research from John Briney and colleagues in 2017 shows this to be a fallacy, with no association shown between schools surveying pupils on their behaviours, and subsequent adoption of those same behaviours by respondents.

So how does this relate to whole school approaches? One key route is via the adoption of a social norms approach. In a nutshell, this builds on the work of Wes Perkins in both the UK and USA (cited in Mentor-ADEPIS, 2013a), and seeks to normalise the positive behaviours rather than the ones we want young people to avoid. Central to this is the notion that regardless of their own behaviour choices, young people are likely to over-estimate the numbers of their peers who engage in the same behaviour. So they will think more of their peers engage in weekly alcohol use, under-age sex, cannabis use, etc. This is often as a result of the numbers of young people who claim to engage in these behaviours in order to gain kudos among their friends and ultimately a higher social standing within that peer group. This is highlighted by research from Amanda Atkinson and colleagues (2016) which highlights the role of social networking sites in displaying and replaying tales of drunken nights out among social networks. A consequence of these misperceptions is to negatively influence future choices around alcohol use – that is, increasing the likelihood of drinking alcohol to 'fit in'. In many ways this represents a modern way of thinking about 'peer pressure'. No longer about the school bully pointing a finger and making a fellow pupil do something against their will, it is more the fear of missing out (FOMO) and the need to fit in which exemplifies this pressure.

ACTIVITY

Public Health England has produced a suite of resources on different health issues to be delivered in schools. These utilise the Rise Above website (see resources given in the appendix) and a network of vloggers who make regular videos on these topics.

One of these encompasses a session plan and video clips on FOMO to be delivered in a health education curriculum. You can find the resources and related links on the Rise Above teacher zone website.

We would hope that delivery of drug and alcohol education in PSHE and health education would seek to address this, but this is limited not just by the issues around the historically non-statutory status of the subject, but also around the general approach to the issues within education and wider youth health policy – namely one that is reactive in its nature. Content has been influenced by increasing awareness around the numbers of young people smoking, drinking and coming to harm as a result. Therefore, the approach becomes more about avoiding the negative behaviours and their consequences. Ultimately this creates an approach which is constantly chasing its tail. It also creates an approach which unwittingly normalises the very behaviours we want young people to avoid, as our starting point is always the negative. If we are to create a more effective model of prevention, we need to give more credence to the behaviours we want young people to *adopt* rather than avoid. The social norm approach seeks to challenge these misperceptions to positively influence future behaviour choices, with PSHE being a key vehicle for the delivery of this. The use of social norms in alcohol and drug education in particular has long been rooted in the notion that young people (and the adults in their lives for that matter) consistently over-estimate the numbers of their peers who are drinking, smoking, taking drugs, and even having sex. This is in part down to that desire to always act older than we are, and doing things which indicate increased maturity. It is also down to how these behaviours are presented in the media – 'they are all doing it' – and these behaviours becoming 'normalised'. Chapter 5 looks at some of the links with this and gaining increased kudos and social recognition in more detail.

Within PSHE then, this means utilising data (either locally from your local public health team or nationally via the NHS Digital published surveys) to highlight the numbers of young people who have *never* drunk alcohol or who are *not* drinking weekly. This means reinforcing the good historical work achieved around tobacco education by promoting the numbers who have never smoked. If we can disrupt the misperception that 'all my mates are doing it so

I need to do it too' we can start to influence the behaviour choices young people are making. Some of the key messages from the national 'Smoking, drinking and drug use in young people' survey which can be flipped include:

- How many pupils have never drunk alcohol?

- How many 15-year-olds are not drinking alcohol weekly?

- How many pupils have never smoked?

- How many 15-year-olds have never tried cannabis?

Any local surveys are also likely to ask similar questions and will add greater relevance for pupils in your school, as well as some specific issues you may want to address such as energy drinks or e-cigarettes. So again, engagement with your local public health teams can be very fruitful here.

Returning to the issues around positive media stories being fudged by relying on stock 'girl on street bench' photos, we also need to think about the imagery used in both lesson materials and wall displays. Further research by Wes Perkins (Perkins, Craig and Perkins, 2011) suggests that regardless of the message we want to convey via text, the brain will look for images first and foremost. So including an image at odds with the message a poster or display may be focused on, can prove problematic and limit the effectiveness of that message. Examples include the age-old technique of a cigarette or alcohol bottle with a line or big red 'x' through it, with Perkins again suggesting the 'x' has little influence on decision making. In many ways the imagery needs to be as boring as possible so as not to distract from the message being conveyed. A good example would be a simple picture of young people alongside a strapline of 'X number of 15-year-olds in London choose not to drink alcohol'.

Smoking and electronic cigarettes

There is little UK guidance around delivering information on e-cigarettes beyond an updated Mentor-ADEPIS briefing produced in 2016, and even since then things have moved on with more recent announcements from Public Health England, who suggested the cancer potency of e-cigarettes to be 0.5 per cent that of traditional tobacco cigarettes (Public Health England, 2018). This suggests that in PSHE and health education we should be taking a balanced view of the role of e-cigarettes. Initial research around uptake amongst young people is still in its infancy and therefore in need of a large pinch of salt when being interpreted. On the one hand, we have seen some suggestions that e-cigarette use is increasing among young people, and in particular for experimental use. On the other hand, however, we can also see expressions of interest in e-cigarettes as a smoking cessation tool. In light of inconsistent uptake of traditional smoking cessation support across the UK, this suggests the harm reduction slant is one worthy of further promotion. Arguably, this is furthered when we consider the issues substance misuse services encounter when working with young cannabis users – that is, the nicotine dependency is not only a secondary issue worthy of further support, but also a key trigger for relapse.

A small-scale study on the views of young people on e-cigarettes conducted in Welsh schools (where elements of health education are statutory already) found some interesting results (Porcellato et al., 2018). These included a distinction between why people use e-cigarettes compared to traditional cigarettes, with the main reason for using the former being as a way to stop smoking, and the latter as a way to 'look cool' and relieve stress. This suggests that messages around the different nature of e-cigarettes to traditional cigarettes are getting through to young people, although whether this is as a result of government advice is less clear. Familial exposure, advertising and treatment of these within the wider media is also likely to be playing a part. What was less clear in the minds of young people was the role of nicotine in this process, although those who had family members who vaped were better informed (Porcellato et al., 2018). With all this in mind, having clear messages delivered through health education becomes more important, and one we hope will be present in English schools post 2020.

ACTIVITY

This activity is safer when delivered to older young people, perhaps aged 14 and over. Present them with some imagery and headlines around e-cigarette use and vaping. The gateway theory versus harm reduction argument can produce a lively debate among young people on the role of e-cigarettes in today's society. One side can argue for the case that they should be banned as they represent a high level of risk of developing dependency and leading to traditional cigarettes, while the other side can argue the case for them as a harm-reducing tool and one which reduces demand on the NHS and social care. Having Public Health England briefing papers and blogs to hand will ensure you have a definitive government response around these, but the purpose of a debate such as this is to further young people's understanding of the pros and cons of drug use, and to be able to debate the facts in a coherent and safe way. These skills will help them when it comes to real-life scenarios and decisions around e-cigarette use and vaping.

On top of the direct impact of e-cigarettes on young people, the issue around familial e-cigarette use is also an important consideration. We know that while smoking prevention campaigns are on the whole an example of a successful whole systems approach to reducing smoking rates nationally, there is also an issue of late presentation to cancer services amongst those left behind and still smoking. This can be considered an unintended consequence of the success of the 'stop smoking' campaigns in that those who still smoke at risky levels are more likely to consider themselves failures, an unwanted burden to the NHS, and therefore present later to treatment for smoking-related illness. In addition, the nature of advertising undertaken by some brands doesn't help with challenging the cynical view. On the whole, they have come across as selling a lifestyle choice rather than a smoking cessation tool. Necessity makes this understandable to a degree while we still await longitudinal studies into harms and benefits of e-cigarette use – but the aggressive nature of some campaigns which bear no resemblance to the product they are selling, and which focus on the perceived cultural capital up for grabs to the potential user, to me only heightens suspicions. And ultimately, this feeds into the confusion around how to tackle them in the classroom.

While we know that the numbers of young people who are smoking traditional tobacco cigarettes have steadily declined – 45 per cent of 11–15-year-olds in 2000 had ever smoked compared to 19 per cent in 2016 – more recently the numbers who have tried e-cigarettes have increased. In 2016, 27 per cent of boys and 25 per cent of girls aged 11–15 reported they had ever tried an e-cigarette, with the figures creeping over 40 per cent when looking at 15-year-olds alone. It should be said that the numbers classing themselves as 'current' e-cigarette users are in single figures, further supporting the idea that their use is more related to experimentation than habitual use or dependency. Indeed, those working with young people increasingly refer to this as young people showing off by performing 'tricks' with the smoke more than anything more sinister.

In spite of the relative low risk of e-cigarettes compared to tobacco, we do need to be careful to not necessarily equate that to being 'risk free'. Ultimately research is still being collated around longer-term harms of vaping nicotine, and similar to other behaviours and substances the risk of dependence is also relevant.

Parents

Engaging parents in elements of alcohol and drug education and prevention has traditionally been very difficult for schools and health professionals. This is despite evidence showing that large numbers of 11–15-year-olds who drink obtain this either directly from parents, or at least via the home environment. Indeed, there are correlations within the areas exhibiting the highest rates of 15-year-olds who drink weekly, with higher rates of young people who say they get their alcohol from the home. While we can't jump to conclusions and claim that one factor causes the other, the correlation certainly means we need to do more in engaging parents in alcohol education and prevention.

Difficulties in engaging parents can be seen in recent research investigating a whole system programme to alcohol education which was trialled in secondary schools in Scotland and Northern Ireland. Despite the involvement of local stakeholders and researchers, the programme only managed to engage around 9 per cent of parents in sessions aimed at supporting them with strategies around talking to their children about alcohol (McKay et al., 2017). This suggests there are many potential barriers to engaging parents which we need to consider. Some of these include:

- *Self-reflection* – the general social acceptance of alcohol means it can be difficult for parents to engage in alcohol education, as the process can prompt them to reflect on their own alcohol use and role in potentially making alcohol available to their children.

- *The continental approach* – the widely held belief that 'giving them a bit now helps them respect it' can be used to both influence and justify certain attitudes towards alcohol within the home. Again, the potential of this being challenged by a school makes it more unlikely for parents to attend designated alcohol sessions.

- *Inter-generational views on school* – parents' personal experiences of school as children themselves will likely influence their engagement as parents too. This is particularly the case in more vulnerable families, which can result in inter-generational distrust of the school environment. As we know that the likelihood of pupils drinking to risky levels increases with the number of risk factors present in their lives, these parents are arguably the ones who would most benefit from engagement yet may be less likely to do so.

- *Timing of sessions* – most sessions are likely to be offered after school which brings further barriers around childcare and fitting around work patterns. These sessions are also sensitive to wider influences such as weather (good or bad), time of year, or even any sporting events which may be happening. I have personal experience of being present at an after-school parent session which clashed with an important England football match. Regardless of personal choice around television and sport-spectating habits of school staff, this is unlikely to help parents attend!

To engage with parents more effectively we therefore need to find ways to overcome these barriers to engagement. Do we necessarily need to be planning set 'events' around these issues? There is certainly an argument for placing things under a broader and more acceptable umbrella of 'child health' rather than just 'alcohol', 'drugs' or even 'mental health'. This softens the edges a bit and becomes a more palatable event for parents to attend and engage with. We often talk about the importance of school health drop-ins being very broad in their naming to attract pupils rather than it being specifically about mental health or sexual health, for example, so we need to think in the same way about engaging parents. An evening of 'alcohol education' for parents is more likely to be perceived as lecturing or telling them how to parent rather than a supportive, practical workshop. This is where the potential wording of 'health education' within the National Curriculum from 2020 will help.

We can also think about how we promote and deliver these messages. With the barriers of timing and inter-generational fear of school, specific standalone sessions are unlikely to be successful (although I accept there are positive examples to counter this!). Therefore, we need to think about using the times when parents are present in schools more effectively. Parent–teacher evenings are ideal examples of this, and these are occasions where we effectively have a potentially captive audience to engage with. This doesn't mean a specific alcohol or health awareness talk has to be planned, more a 'light touch' display or stand with information presented, along with teaching or pastoral staff ready to answer any questions about the school's approach. In this example, parents are effectively approaching school staff rather than the other way around, thus making the whole process less daunting and less confrontational. The interaction becomes a supportive and informational one rather than 'the school telling me how to parent'. A particularly powerful way to run this type of approach is to use some pupils in this process too – possibly using any youth health champions schools have, or at the very least, school council members. The use of pupils validates the information given and gives more opportunities to hear about why they value the role of alcohol and health education in their lives.

At very simple levels, the use of normative information has further potential in these environments. While we know more about how young people over-estimate the numbers of their peers engaging in unhealthy behaviours and coping mechanisms, when it comes to parents this evidence is far more anecdotal. However, the way young people and alcohol is portrayed by the media suggests this trend of over-estimation is likely to be prevalent in parents too. The principles of sticking to the message and keeping imagery very simple and neutral is of utmost importance here, while focusing on alcohol and tobacco use is likely to resonate more than drug use – 'that's not my child' is likely to be the response to the latter. Despite this, there is still the need to have relevant and up-to-date literature and information on drug use as much as alcohol use here. Local public health teams in the UK will be able to help schools access the most relevant information locally in relation to this.

POINTS FOR PRACTICE

Key points for planning of alcohol and tobacco education include:

- Instead of referring to the numbers of young people engaging in drinking or smoking behaviour, focus on those who do not. This social norm approach challenges the commonly held misperception among young people that 'all my mates are doing it, so I should too'.

- In the UK, if your local public health team cannot help with local data on this, use information from the national 'Smoking, drinking and drug use among young people' survey from NHS Digital.

- Evidence doesn't support the view that e-cigarette use among young people leads to smoking traditional tobacco cigarettes.

- E-cigarettes are accepted to be less carcinogenic than tobacco cigarettes, although further research is required into long-term impacts of use.

Further drawing from some of the key issues in this chapter, some suggestions to engage parents include:

- Placing alcohol and drug education in the wider remit of 'health education'. This can minimise the impact of parents thinking it is not relevant for them as 'that's not my child'.

- Use parent evenings more effectively for a 'light touch' approach. This can mean those parents who are unlikely to attend standalone sessions due to work or childcare commitments can still be targeted.

- Use of pupils to engage with parents. This can add more credence to the message as it is coming from pupils themselves, in addition to overcoming parental fear of schools and teachers.

– Use of social norms in these activities. This can help challenge misperceptions around young people and alcohol use.

– The continental approach of giving them some alcohol early so they respect it in later life is not supported by evidence. The UK's Chief Medical Officers recommend an alcohol-free lifestyle before age 15.

CHAPTER 5

Body Image and IPEDs

Issues around body image and the impact of self-perception on young people's mental health is a high-priority issue, culminating in a focus in the government green paper of 2017 and reports by the Children's Commissioner for England, the Chief Medical Officer for England, and the House of Commons Education Select Committee. Hand in hand with discussions on young people and body image is often the role of social media, almost as an umbrella term for social networking sites, online news outlets and wider youth culture as played out in online 'spaces'. This chapter seeks to provide a possible theoretical framework to help increase understanding of the underlying drivers behind this issue, going beyond the simplistic knee jerk reaction of blaming the online media and the online social networking industries. This chapter will also touch on some of the negative coping mechanisms which schools and young people's services may notice, including eating disorders and image and performance-enhancing drugs (IPEDs) – these include substances such as steroids and diet pills.

Getting theoretical – Bourdieu

One possible perspective to use when exploring how body image becomes a key issue for young people is through the work of Pierre Bourdieu, a French anthropologist and sociologist who explored the different ways cultural tastes become accepted by different groups within society, and how certain forms of 'capital' are held in different levels of esteem by people within those groups. He framed 'capital' as effectively a unit of cultural taste which comes in different forms – effectively we may use the term 'kudos' to describe this in more simplistic ways. Bourdieu (2010) refers to different types of capital as:

- *Economic* – rooted in the status afforded to someone according to their wealth.

- *Social* – rooted in the social status individuals may find themselves in, closely related to social class, employment and where they live.

- *Cultural* – rooted in the status afforded to someone according to their position within a certain element of culture. This can be in a very wide sense in terms of popular culture, or also through subcultures. So someone with a lot of knowledge or understanding of popular culture can have high cultural capital among some groups, but this may be considered low capital by someone who identifies with another culture or subculture. Contrasting styles of music can be a good example here where a fan of hip-hop music may have high cultural capital within a group of like-minded people, but low capital among those who prefer 'indie' music. These individual tastes are important in how levels of capital – or kudos – are given and received.

Arguably cultural capital is of greater importance to young people as they use elements of youth culture to explore, create and experience their own identities. Bourdieu has another concept for how as individuals we interact with these forms of capital – the habitus. This refers to how we use our bodies as vehicles to display the levels of capital we have and how others around us interpret that. This can be through clothing, hairstyles, jewellery, tattoos, how we walk and talk, the spaces we like to be in, the people we like to socialise with. Over time we can see how the process of constructing this 'habitus' for young people has changed. Consider how young people dressed and acted in each decade since the 1960s and we can see how what is considered high cultural and social capital has changed according to what is 'popular' at the time. In this way, we can make the links between Bourdieu's concepts of the habitus and exchange of capital, and what we now term 'body image'. What types of 'body' (habitus) are considered by young people to have more capital imbued in them and therefore become more desirable? A simple body map activity with different groups in different parts of the country may give us very different results. Some may interpret a certain hairstyle or body shape as being of high capital in Manchester, whereas young people in

Cornwall may see a different body shape or style of clothing as being more desirable for attaining that high capital from their peers. Indeed, I have done this very activity with people in the same service and this has given up different elements of culture they hold important when creating their own 'habitus'.

What does this mean in practice? For some, a valid conclusion to come to is that if young people have different ideas of how they want to look and carry themselves, different ideas of what their habitus is, then we can't have a 'one size fits all' solution to that. It can't just be about asking clothing companies to use diverse models (male and female) in advertising campaigns. That is a reactive way of dealing with the issue, and one fixed on one facet of the phenomenon. It has to be more about appreciating the fact young people are viewed as consumers to a much higher extent by the wider cultural industries than previous generations. Greater disposable income and increased ways for advertisers to directly reach younger audiences has seen to that. So any approaches to protect young people from experiencing negative body image need to reflect this. We can start by helping them explore how and why it is that they feel different 'bodies' hold different levels of capital within peer groups, and the changing nature of that over time. We can help them to be 'critical consumers' by thinking about what is behind a company's decision to market their product in such a way. The Dove Self-Esteem Project has been supporting schools in this for a number of years (Unilever, 2018), and I have also seen how schools have taken on advice from Natasha Devon MBE and others to support pupils to be aware of the 'white writing' hidden in commercials.

ACTIVITIES

Body map – draw an outline of a body on a large sheet of paper and label the things young people feel are important to 'show' to get recognition. Ask adults to do a similar one for when they were teenagers and compare and contrast the results. How important are these things?

'White writing' (credit to Natasha Devon!) – choose a selection of adverts for beauty products from YouTube. Allow young people to watch each one and then repeat the same advert, pausing when the white writing appears at the bottom of the screen. It normally

contains information about any claims made and any disclaimers too. Are the sample sizes from any surveys really big enough to support the claims made? Does 67 per cent really mean that most people agree this product is good for their skin? Prompt young people to be critical about the information in the white writing and how that has changed their view of the product.

Getting theoretical – Foucault

When it comes to specifically looking at the impact of social networking sites we can also lean on another French sociologist for insight into this. Michel Foucault (1991) wrote extensively on a range of social issues and phenomena, with many of them relating back to the notion of power exerted by some areas of society over others. In relation to body image and Bourdieu's idea of the habitus, I'd like to explore Foucault's analogy of the 'panopticon' as a method of social control. The panopticon was a structure devised by Jeremy Bentham at the turn of the eighteenth and nineteenth centuries as a way of maintaining discipline in prisons at the time. Effectively the panopticon was a tower built in the middle of an open space which was then surrounded by cells built into a circular outer wall. The tower in the centre would contain the prison guards, from where they could observe all inmates at any one time. The trick here is that the cells would remain lit so inmates were always visible to the guards, while the tower was shrouded in darkness meaning the inmates could not see the guards or if they were being observed at any given moment. The panopticon therefore became a tool for modifying behaviour of inmates not by direct observation as such, but by creating the illusion that at any given time they *could* be being observed without them knowing it. That knowledge alone was enough to create a fear of observation and discipline which resulted in self-regulation of behaviour.

Foucault conceptualised this within the closed prison environment as a form of 'anonymous' power being exerted over the inmates – where they didn't know who or if they were being surveilled. In effect this power meant the inmate behaviour was being controlled by the state. Foucault then explored how this principle is used in wider society, initially by the state as a method of control over its population, but also in more subtle ways too. One example we can see is in the use of things like speed cameras on the roads. Regardless of the law around speed limits, drivers often don't know if they are turned on and out of fear of the repercussions will self-regulate their speed. In this way the government is seeking to produce safer roads not necessarily by direct punishment – that is, prosecuting those who are caught speeding – but by making drivers regulate their own driving speed. That is a fairly innocuous but still debatably successful way of utilising panoptocism in wider society. Indeed, some have already applied this to modern technology in the workplace (Zuboff, 1988), and we can also think of things like CCTV in schools. Is that an effective way of controlling pupil behaviour or another example of limiting human agency? Are pupils learning self-regulation or just a fear of discipline and punishment? Either way we can use these ideas to help think about the role of SNS in promoting different types of body image.

We could all name some examples of popular social networking sites among young people, but by the time this book goes to print and you are reading this, those same young people will probably have moved on to use another set of sites! If anything, that highlights the need not to focus on the sites themselves, although they undoubtedly do need to up their game in terms of social responsibility, but to focus more on the processes common to each. If the original panopticon was about prison guards and inmates, we can arguably relate that to the social networking site and its users. At any given time, a young person is not aware who may or may not be viewing their posts or timeline. This drives behaviour not in the direction of avoiding behaviour, but actually exhibiting it. As young people are continually trying to gain that cultural capital among their peers, they therefore are not stopping posting images and updates at all, but rather are more inclined to do so more often 'just in case' one of their peers is online and viewing their timeline. So the absence of postings is likely to result in a loss of capital, and an increase in posts result in an enhanced possibility for gaining cultural capital. Can we therefore start to use this as our starting point for understanding and talking to young people about the role of social networking sites in how they construct their identities? Is too much importance being given to exchanging capital with the hundreds of followers they may have online over and above the potential for exchanging capital face to face? In many ways this has links with core skills such as creating and maintaining strong friendships. If we focus on that is there less need to seek approval from the panoptic online collection of friends and followers?

Foucault explored more explicit ways these processes occur in society, and their role in eliminating social agency – effectively an individual's right to control their own actions and make their own decisions, whether good or bad. Foucault extends this exertion of power with the idea of 'the gaze', which relates to a more conscious notion of panopticism and is less about controlling behaviour and more about how it governs how we strive for certain ideals to gain recognition from others. A good example is how many things in society are driven by what a stereotypical male may think – effectively a 'male gaze'. This can influence how people dress and the way that is perceived and commented on – similar to how Bourdieu described his thinking. In many ways this can therefore be viewed hand in hand with how young people may strive for that high cultural capital. This also has some cross-over with social norms, which was discussed in more detail in Chapter 4, which can further skew wider perceptions of what is the predominant ideal body.

ACTIVITY

What is me? – on a sheet of paper ask a young person to draw a spider diagram with them in the middle and all the things important to them branching out from it. Discuss why each of these things is important to them, and whether social media influences each one. Try to circle each one with a green pen if it is influenced positively or a red one if influenced negatively. You may also get some that are 50/50 or 70/30! This gives a visual aid for how their lives may be over-influenced by an online 'identity' and helps them identify areas they could change – effectively make more green.

Impact – gender as 'performance'?

Judith Butler (1993) has suggested that society views the concept of gender as a fixed, slow-moving idea of what it is to be male and female, and arguably we could add other genders into that now too. If we view how gender is expressed as a 'performance', we can start to challenge those fixed notions of gender – and sexuality – and challenge the making of these under a heterosexual male 'gaze'. So with young people, can we support them in thinking outside of these very boundaried ideals of what it is to perform our gender? Can we move on from viewing those who wear their hair in a certain style, who choose to wear dresses or suits, who paint their nails or wear make-up as representations of just being male or female? It seems to me that those in the public eye who challenge these ideals are seen as more acceptable due to the fact they live different lives in that world of celebrity. When someone chooses to perform their gender outside of that male and female binary in more public spaces that somehow is less acceptable to society. Promoting acceptance of these different performances is what can not only support those young people who do not see themselves as conforming to strict ideas of what it is to be male or female, but can also help them realise that their own differences are not a cause for internalised shame or guilt.

If we want to explore the wider impact of these pressures on young people, then we can start to appreciate how the role of social networking sites can be detrimental to young people's wellbeing. Research has suggested this is particularly the case around how young people use alcohol to construct their identities online in online spaces (Atkinson et al., 2016). In this paper, the authors argue that young people use social networking sites to exchange cultural capital closely linked to alcohol use. So this could be by creating and retelling stories they hope their peers will find funny, while at the same time displaying how they are 'OK' with alcohol consumption and can 'handle their drink'. This is especially important when we consider that young people show increased sensitivity to social information and influences compared to adults. The nature of the developing adolescent brain outlined in Chapter 3 means we shouldn't really be surprised at this, and should therefore be able to bring this into approaches to working with young people on the influence of social networking sites. Recent research from Yvonne Kelly at UCL has further suggested that there are gender differences to these online interactions, with girls being more likely to make comparisons between themselves and their peers than boys – perhaps feeding into negative cycles of self-esteem and body image. On the other hand, boys may be more likely to interact in online spaces through gaming rather than social networking sites per se. Similar gender expectations can play out with substance use, where boys are more likely to externalise their use as a way to show off and gain capital from wider peer networks, while girls may be more likely to internalise this either on an individual level or within much smaller networks. While we may not necessarily be looking for gendered sessions on this within health education, it does suggest that approaches need to cover all elements of online interaction and communication rather than just specific sites.

If we have a more informed understanding of what drives how young people view themselves and their bodies, we can make more effective choices about how we support them in the classroom through PSHE, as well as the wider system of support when things do go wrong. This practising of positive coping can be a proactive way of preventing issues arising such as eating disorders, over-eating, or image-enhancing drugs such as steroids and slimming pills. Some of the key factors to consider around each of these will be looked at in the remainder of this chapter.

Eating disorders and over-exercising

A common driver behind the development of eating disorders and over-exercising is not only the misplaced need to conform to a certain ideal body shape, but more importantly the element of control involved in these behaviours. In this sense we need to appreciate that wider mental health issues are at play which, when combined with poor body image, can result in the adoption of negative coping mechanisms. We also need to reflect on the fact that young people are more likely to express satisfaction with their bodies when they are underweight. Therefore, they are more likely to apply greater social capital to those body styles. We might not be surprised to learn that girls are most dissatisfied when they have excess body weight, but perhaps more worrying is that they still express dissatisfaction even when they are of a 'normal', healthy weight. This distortion of what is seen as acceptable, healthy and 'normal' can therefore be a powerful influence on the adoption of unhealthy ways of both coping with unwanted feelings around their body image, and also how they strive for greater acceptance within their peer groups – even when this is a misguided view. Figure 5.1 shows how these issues are played out in the numbers of 15-year-olds who are unhappy with the way they look. Most worrying are the numbers who do not identify as heterosexual for whom this is a greater issue, as displayed in Figure 5.2.

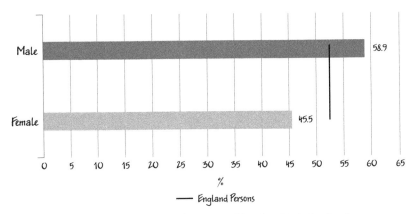

Figure 5.1: Percentage of 15-year-olds who think they're the right size – England 2014/15 – data partitioned by sex
Source: adapted from the What About YOUth? Survey, 2015

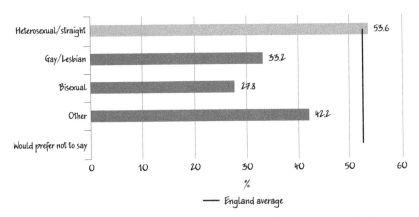

Figure 5.2: Percentage of 15-year-olds who think they're the right size – England 2014/15 – data partitioned by sexuality – five categories
Source: adapted from the What About YOUth? Survey, 2015

If we relate this to the average class of 30 15-year-olds, only 16 are likely to think they are the right size. If all that class identified as gay or lesbian, only ten would think they are the right size. If they all identified as bisexual that would drop to eight (all via What About YOUth survey, 2015). This suggests that those pupils who may be exploring their sexuality are more sensitive to the idea of 'body shape' outlined throughout this chapter. In this sense, I don't necessarily mean sensitive in a purely emotional way, but more in how they may be influenced by body image and how it subsequently impacts on their own wellbeing. These pupils may be more tuned in to how they perceive and construct their own 'habitus', particularly if their body image doesn't just fail to conform to traditional gender stereotypes, but more importantly is one which fails to conform to heterosexual ideals – that is, media representations of girls attracting boys and boys attracting girls. This is what Butler is getting at around the idea of gender as a performance rather than just something we 'have'. The perceived lack of connection with what societal norms say it is to be a 15-year-old can therefore have detrimental impacts on mental health and ideals of self-worth and self-esteem.

Regardless of gender and/or sexual orientation, this is where elements of control over eating and exercising routines can be adopted in unhealthy ways to achieve perceived wider peer acceptance, either in large year groups or possibly in smaller subcultural groups. This should therefore suggest that within health education we should be looking less at the pitfalls of specific eating disorders, but more at the skills needed to help pupils feel confident in challenging these so-called 'ideal bodies'. This could mean:

- *Increased media literacy* – developing skills in questioning why a certain picture was chosen to accompany a news report, or why a company has chosen to advertise its product in such a way.

- *Increased self-worth* – developing skills around identifying and celebrating the uniqueness of us all as individuals. These are things that bring strength to our character and personality rather than a weakness for being 'different'.

- *Understanding the impact of social media* – developing skills around minimising the 'fear of missing out' by not engaging on social networking sites. This could include challenging how many filters or practice shots are needed before an Instagram post by celebrities. (The Dove Self-Esteem Project is an excellent resource for supporting pupils in gaining these skills.)

From a pastoral support perspective, those pupils who are struggling with a diagnosed or suspected eating disorder need elements of understanding and a place to be listened to in school rather than direct challenging of their behaviour (Knightsmith, 2015). In many cases an eating disorder is something which has developed over time, and as such cannot be simply stopped overnight. Yet this contradicts the protective social parent in those universal-level professionals which wants to snap our fingers to make everything OK. The increased need around these issues is reflected by increased focus on the development of specific and responsive local eating disorder services within Future in Mind and Local Transformation Plans. It is a strong example of where therapeutic support can be offered by other health professionals on the school site rather than by school staff themselves. Underpinning this, young people are looking more for day-to-day 'ordinary magic' from those whom they see on a daily basis in school. This means not necessarily offering big interventions, but subtly changing the way we interact with pupils (and colleagues) in small and manageable ways. So offering that time and space to just 'listen' – without judgement or the fear of 'we have to do something now' – can have greater impact than we give it credit for. We might think about offering small extensions to deadlines to relieve pressure on those pupils who are struggling and accessing support elsewhere. If they see school as their 'safe place' then how can we help them feel better about this at pressure points like Monday mornings and Friday afternoons? These things are often overlooked in favour of the 'intervention', but it is often the most powerful way of just being there for those who need it. Chapter 9 offers some practical ideas on how this can be done.

Contagion

Exposure to unhealthy coping mechanisms such as disordered eating, substance use or self-harm, either within peer groups or via the media, can have negative consequences and increase the likelihood of young people engaging in them (Knightsmith, 2015). This concept is referred to as contagion – effectively meaning the unhealthy coping can be spread among a group of peers. This can sometimes become more likely if there is a popular programme depicting this (such as the Netflix series *13 Reasons Why*), or high-profile news reports. Any increases in incidence of unhealthy coping around these times is not just related to young people trying these things for the first time; it needs to be remembered that these occasions can be very triggering for those who have previously self-harmed or used drugs as a coping mechanism. For these young people, increased media coverage and people talking about it can be a very difficult time and result in relapse to that very behaviour they may have fought so hard to overcome. It is a key thing which is commonly overlooked on awareness days – both local and national. It is in these situations where contagion can be a possibility.

However, a common misconception around this process is that by talking about these risky behaviours in school we are making them more likely to happen. If anything, it can be argued that contagion becomes more likely if these unhealthy coping mechanisms are not discussed, or are talked about in unsafe ways or unsafe environments. An example could be a one-off session on self-harm or body image as part of a drop-day, with no opportunity for wider discussions or exploring healthy alternatives. Again, this can be more likely around high-profile media coverage which can result in knee jerk responses around a need to deliver 'something' on the subject. This can do more harm than good as it raises awareness without developing skills or consolidating learning (I have a big problem with high-profile calls to 'raise awareness' on issues for this very reason). As highlighted in the case study at the end of this chapter, young people can really benefit from hearing about positive coping from their peers. In many ways, this represents a healthy contagion – spreading the positive behaviour rather than the negative. It is by talking about self-harm and substance use in a safe environment with confidence with school staff that opportunities for this healthy contagion can occur. Again this takes us back to the importance of staff training within the whole school approach, and finding that staff member who feels confident and comfortable in talking about some of these difficult topics. An example could be the use of online webinars from reputable sources, such as the Charlie Waller Memorial Trust.

Image-enhancing drugs

Some young people with low self-esteem, low self-worth and a poor image of themselves may turn to artificial ways of improving their outward image. This can take the form of using things like steroids to build up muscle definition and tone, or slimming pills as a shortcut to lose excess weight and therefore achieve that more desirable body shape. The often secretive nature of these behaviour choices again makes prevalence difficult to accurately ascertain, yet anecdotal reports from around the country tell us that young people are turning to these substances (Maddison and Handley-Ward, 2018). Again, underpinning these choices are some of the external social and developmental forces and pressures discussed already in this chapter. The desire to attain a body shape and image which holds greater social capital among peers, the panoptic fear of being overlooked on social networking sites, or the need to perform a socially acceptable version of gender can all be influencing factors. The resulting coping mechanism can therefore be understood as a function of these factors and an inability to choose a healthier alternative to restore good mental health.

The use of steroids is more commonly found in young males, often sourced through attending gyms but, as with many other pharmaceutical drugs, through online sources too. Effectively these substances are not just about directly increasing muscle size per se, but are more about improving the rate and quality of muscle recovery from workouts. This in turn brings about increased muscle size and definition in a relatively short period of time. Steroid use is a very controlled practice, so in many ways we can draw similarities with other controlling behaviours as coping mechanisms, including restrictive diets and self-harming behaviours. The controlled practice arises from a need to follow a regime of periods taking steroids, followed by planned breaks to enable the body to restore some hormonal balance and restrict unwanted side effects. Some of these side effects are increased aggression (so called 'roid rage'), poor skin quality and acne, reduced sexual desire, and in young males the development of secondary female characteristics ('man boobs') as a result of the body changing its levels of hormone production in response to increased steroid levels regularly being present. This strict control and regime around steroid use is something young users will often get from those who are supplying steroids in gym environments. These individuals are far removed from the mediated view of the street dealer, and can actually be seen by younger gym goers as role models. In some cases, they are seen as 'brokers of masculinity' – that is, they are the means by which a young man with low body confidence can attain a body image with perceived greater cultural and social capital. This is one of the reasons why steroid use is more difficult to spot and support than someone using more illicit substances. So again, finding ways to disrupt the perception of what the 'perfect' male body is should be of increased importance in health education. This returns us to the skills we can develop through challenging those ideals.

By the same token, rather than seeking to gain weight or muscle mass to improve personal body image, some young people seek to use slimming pills as a way to lose weight and body mass. These substances are not just restricted in a stereotypical way to young girls either. Although these substances have traditionally been used in a more drastic way by those who are overweight or obese, increasingly we are seeing use among those with a healthy weight who still feel the need to lose weight to achieve that more desirable body shape. In many cases these substances can be marketed not as 'drugs', but as 'fat burners' or even 'supplements'. These substances can include laxatives to stimulate bowel movements, ephedrine to stimulate the breakdown and removal of fat either stored in the body or eaten in food, and clenbuterol to increase metabolism and thus minimise the amount of fat stored in the body. A fat-loss drug called DNP is being increasingly linked to harmful side effects, with its main reason for use being to prevent energy being stored as fat. However, Public Health England has recently responded to an increase in deaths associated with DNP use by releasing its own warning, including risks of seizures, kidney and other organ damage and muscle damage. One of the issues is a common one with most illicit substances – that of no control over contents and dosage between pills. In this sense, we can see how the inclusion of generic medicine education can also have a protective role around these substances – that is, whether we know what a drug contains, what a safe dose is, and the need for safety offered by the process of prescribing drugs rather than obtaining them through illicit means. The normalised view of the 'dealer' also has implications here, particularly with the increased numbers of people, young and old, obtaining drugs via the internet. This can be seen as a more socially acceptable practice as drug use is only illicit and 'other' when bought from a back-street dealer. Challenging these views is again important if we are to support healthy and safe choices. The section on risk in Chapter 7 is of particular relevance here too, and has some useful suggestions for incorporating this in a health education curriculum.

So when approaching issues around body image and image-enhancing substances, we need to remember that social media plays a prominent part in young people constructing and playing out their own identities. However, this runs the risk of us laying the blame solely at the door of social media sites rather than acknowledging what it is which leads young people to put increased emphasis on them. It is through this that we can seek to challenge and support their use of these sites in constructing their identities in healthy ways. That view also overlooks the positive role which social media can play in the lives of young people who are struggling. For those who find social situations difficult, these online spaces can help them make positive connections and access support in ways they would otherwise find too hard to do.

Poor body image should be viewed as a result of the interplay between the perceived benefits of a certain type of 'body', and how young people find opportunities to display this to peers for approval and acceptance. By viewing it in this way, we can appreciate how focusing on key friendship skills within health education and wider pastoral support can help minimise the impact of 'the gaze' on individual behaviour choices. Within this, finding ways to challenge what young people commonly think are the 'perfect' body types can be a powerful preventative tool, instead of focusing on specific risks of using image-enhancing drugs, controlled eating or over-exercising alone.

POINTS FOR PRACTICE

Rick Bradley developed 'Mind and Body', an award-winning early intervention programme for young people focused on preventing the risks associated with self-harm. Their teams regularly work with young people around body image, poor mental health and subsequent unhealthy coping mechanisms and he has these key points for both schools and those delivering early intervention programmes to consider:

- One of the most impactful things is the importance of group settings and having young people hearing from other young people about their opinions and experiences. Feedback from participants tells us this is key to the success of the programme as it helps them realise that they are not alone in feeling anxious, reducing feelings of stigma and isolation.

- Among teachers and other professionals, there can be a fear of 'contagion' if young people are to be having these discussions in groups – if they are hearing from others who have experience of self-harm, will this not make them more likely to do the same? This has not been the case with our groups but it is an understandable concern and is something to be mindful of. The process therefore needs to be delivered by trained and confident staff experienced in both the relevant issues and working with young people in small groups. This helps maintain a safe environment for these issues to be explored. Giving additional space for individual discussions also helps ensure young people have an appropriate place to share more personal concerns that might require a specific focus. For some, this may mean resisting the pull to do 'something' and to seek relevant CPD first – remember there is potential to do more harm by facilitating these groups when not confident or appropriately trained.

- One of the reasons young people find this approach most useful is the current lack of time for exploring why we experience poor mental health, and how to manage this, within the PSHE curriculum. This is more the case for self-harm and body image rather than substance use, as the externalised bravado (similar to 'cultural capital' as Bourdieu would put it) associated with drug use is removed. Body image and weight issues can elicit more internalised feelings of shame and guilt which are therefore harder to explore in unsafe or time-limited environments, so supporting these discussions is really important in helping young people manage their feelings and associated coping strategies.

- We also need to remember that different coping strategies are used by different people – whether positive or negative. So we can't therefore apply a 'one size fits all' approach, which leads us back to promoting the skills young people need to identify when they are experiencing poor mental health, and how they can restore good mental health using healthy coping strategies. An example could be how the use of Xanax or other drugs may be stumbled upon as a coping strategy, rather than young people seeking them out to specifically help them reduce anxiety. This isn't the perspective put forward by the media so we need to be sensitive to that. However, this does also mean that young people can be supported to stumble across healthy ways of coping, bringing us back to the power of hearing from other young people's experiences and what works for them in healthy ways.

Rick can be found on Twitter @RickBrad1ey.

CHAPTER 6

Energy Drinks and Smart Drugs

The rise of caffeinated and energy drinks has blurred the lines around what we consider harmful substance use. This is particularly the case with the ubiquitous nature of caffeine consumption amongst all levels of society, unlike the deviant and 'other' label attached to the illicit drug user or alcoholic. In this way, 'smart' drugs also fall into the same bracket, and this chapter seeks to explore some of the key issues surrounding their use, informing approaches to them through health education and wider school policy.

Like many of its illicit counterparts, caffeine is a naturally occurring substance which humans have been consuming for hundreds of years. Its presence in drinks derived from plants such as tea and coffee mean many of us rarely leave the house without using it, and continue to do so throughout our working and leisure time. It plays a big part, therefore, not only in our daily routines, but also as a central part of some traditions, cultures and even health campaigns – for instance taking time for 'a cuppa' to help promote talking more about our mental health. The Time to Change campaign even goes so far as to brand the tea bags themselves! Caffeine is also a common component of many over-the-counter medicines, and in recent years is part of an expanded commercial energy drinks industry. Along with alcohol and nicotine it enjoys special dispensation within the Psychoactive Substances Act which allows it to be bought and sold (and used) without fear of arrest or legal sanctions. While alcohol has guidelines around consumption (for example the use of 'units' for over 18s; and Chief Medical Officer guidance for under 18s), caffeine has no such guidance around so-called safe limits. But tea and coffee drinking is so ingrained in British and European culture – and beyond – so why should it?

For a start, high consumption of caffeine can have unwanted side effects such as anxiety, restlessness, excessive muscle twitching and serious stomach complaints. In some cases, psychological dependence can also occur which brings about symptoms of withdrawal when someone stops using it. I have many experiences of talking about this in schools to teachers and being met with knowing nods and glances from those who have ever left home or the staff room without their morning 'fix'! The cultural acceptance of caffeine and its lack of perceived harm means these conversations can be had in jest without any fear of the social demonising illicit drugs are likely to bring. Yet the impact of withdrawals can be just as difficult to overcome and manage. Headaches, tiredness, irritability, always looking for that next espresso. Yet again, we often laugh these experiences off as it is 'only caffeine', forgetting its impact on the body as a stimulant. Just like smoking, people claiming it helps them relax is not down to the impact of the substance on the body, more its role in dampening withdrawal symptoms and cravings, along with the process of stopping what you are doing and sitting down to enjoy it.

The increased focus on caffeine in adolescence has come about with its presence in energy or high-caffeine soft drinks, and its subsequent popularity with adolescents. So-called 'energy' drinks often contain high levels of caffeine, sugar and other ingredients – often with dubiously stated health benefits (Mentor-ADEPIS, 2013b). Unfortunately, little national data is collected on caffeine or energy drink use – possibly as the reliability of responses is quite shaky as the caffeine content of these drinks (as well as tea and coffee) is variable, along with a lack of understanding around what drinks actually contain high levels of caffeine. However, some local pupil surveys do collect this data and can be quite insightful. Some European datasets have suggested almost a quarter of primary school aged children have drunk energy drinks (via Mentor-ADEPIS, 2013b). This figure rises to around 7 in 10 when it comes to UK teenagers, with more boys generally consuming them than girls.

Issues arising from energy drink consumption

Along with earlier stated issues around pupils drinking energy drinks, lack of sleep and poor behaviour are perhaps the most prominent issues arising from their use. In terms of sleep, we know there is an inverse relationship between amount of caffeine consumed and length of time sleeping in adolescence. Alongside our awareness of the importance of sleep for the developing young brain, we know sleep also has a positive role to play in maintaining good mental health.

For many schools, the issues around consumption of energy drinks are more about their use in and around school times. On top of noticing a growing litter problem, anecdotal evidence suggests increased use in the mornings, often as a substitute for breakfast. We can see how this can produce a negative spiral as increased use leads to decreased sleep, leading to sleeping in late and skipping breakfast, leading to increased morning use, and so on. Additionally, issues can arise from off-premises consumption during break and lunch times – especially for those older pupils with the increased responsibility afforded to them by being allowed offsite in the first place. All in all, this lack of nutritious meals, alongside the stimulant effect of high-caffeine and sugar-containing drinks, has its impacts within the classroom. The stimulant effect can bring about that inability to sit still and the displaying of low-level disruptive behaviours, exacerbated by the loss of inhibitions brought about through increased stimulation. Once that has subsided, the old adage of 'what comes up must come down' comes into play. This energy crash can result in increased feelings of lethargy and lack of motivation, again alongside low-level disruptive behaviour. This cycle can therefore impact on that individual's capacity to learn over the course of a morning or afternoon session, with direct impact on attainment resulting from the adoption of these routines.

Approaches within health education and wider school policy

In recent years, UK supermarkets have taken it upon themselves to impose bans on under 18s buying energy drinks. In many cases this is a blanket ban on all drinks coming under a wide definition rather than those containing a certain amount of caffeine. In some early cases this was in response to direct requests from local schools who were noticing the impact of increased consumption on pupil behaviour and attainment, as well as a playground littered with empty cans and bottles. While this is a welcome development from large companies in the industry, this negates the numbers of newsagents and smaller outlets who do not subscribe to such a ban. For some schools, rather than just approaching them as a senior leadership team, more success has been brought about by pupils and school councils approaching local retailers to ask them to adopt responsible selling practices around school times. What can't be forgotten though, is that the decreased profit margins of these smaller outlets means voluntarily banning under 18s from buying energy drinks can be counterproductive from a business perspective. The end of this chapter has a case study and resources suggesting how the issue of energy drinks can be approached, along with the use of a dedicated Mentor-ADEPIS briefing paper for schools (2013b).

The use of 'smart drugs' (PCEs)

A more recent phenomenon – previously presumed to be restricted to higher education institutions and high-powered and pressurised jobs such as surgeons – is the use of so-called 'smart drugs' which have been subject to increased use worldwide. The use of smart drugs, or pharmacological cognitive enhancers (PCE), to give them their full title, commonly blurs the boundaries between illicit and licit drug use in a similar way to caffeine and energy drinks in that those who use them do not conform to the societal norm of a drug user. However, while energy drink use can be seen in those with increased social risk factors and wider determinants of health, PCE use is more often seen in otherwise healthy individuals. The fact that the reasons for use are initially different from more recreational drugs such as alcohol, cannabis or cocaine, results from their specific role in improving cognition – and ultimately academic performance. This position also means they are unlikely to become the concern of GPs or local drug services as their use has been focused on those 'healthy' individuals who are less likely to come to lasting harm or require medical attention. Common substances coming under the category of PCE include modafinil, Ritalin, and piracetam, with many of them bringing about stimulant-like effects. These can sometimes lead the user to assume the PCE is having a direct impact on academic performance when, in fact, this improvement is a result of the stimulant effect of the substance. Indeed, there is little conclusive evidence to support the effectiveness of these substances as purely enhancers of cognition or brain power (Battleday and Brem, 2015). Where that evidence has been conducted, it is normally among university students. For some, there is controversy over the use of these drugs in their intended treatments, for conditions such as ADHD (see, for example, Cortese, 2016).

The lure of these substances around exam time therefore becomes increasingly obvious for those pupils under increased pressure of high academic expectations. As such, their use can also be seen within a wider umbrella of low self-esteem, high expectations from others, and a high fear of failure. In many ways, therefore, the most appropriate activities for prevention are those which boost those elements rather than pushing the risks of PCE use in isolation. The perceived ease of obtaining them is also a consideration, in particular through online channels and the so called 'dark web'. However, for those who do look to PCEs, adverse effects include poor appetite, increased anxiety, mood swings and poor sleeping patterns. In rare cases, worsening psychiatric harms can develop, as well as skin complaints specifically associated with modafinil use. Again, some of these effects we may expect in anyone experiencing wider mental distress, so general approaches aimed at developing healthy coping mechanisms and promoting positive mental health are likely to impact on pupils at risk of PCE use too. We should also be wary though how the profile of those using PCEs means they are less likely to come to the attention of pastoral services and wider pupil support teams, with any detrimental impacts of their use being largely hidden and unseen – in many ways similar to those engaging in self-harming behaviours.

IN PRACTICE – A CASE STUDY ON CAFFEINE AND ENERGY DRINKS

In the spirit of social norms, a successful partnership between a local health trust, secondary school, and water company focused not on the 'dangers' of high caffeine consumption, but more on promoting the benefits of drinking water. This initiative included lesson content which on the one hand spent some time on the impacts of too much caffeine on pupils, but on the other hand consistently aligned this with the benefits of drinking just water – thus normalising the healthy behaviour rather than the unhealthy alternative. Again, pupil voice was a common theme throughout the resource, in terms of encouraging the process of identifying specific need within an individual school, through to engaging with local retailers and the use of pupils themselves in advertising material around the school.

Following best practice, this was delivered as part of a wider whole school approach to the issue, including specific wording within school policy, staff training, restrictions on soft drinks in both pupils and staff vending machines, and targeted workshops for those pupils who either self-identified or were identified by staff as consuming high levels of energy drinks. The use of pupil surveys enabled the school to measure the impact of this approach, as well as anecdotal evidence from staff and pupils on classroom behaviour and playground litter. Within PSHE, pupils explored not only some unknown risks around excess caffeine consumption, but also what makes adopting healthier alternatives such as water easier. They also explored issues around litter, impact on fellow pupils in the classroom, how to support friends who may be drinking too much caffeine, and also engaging with local newsagents around responsible selling of energy and high-caffeine drinks. Perhaps most importantly, meaningful outcome measures were used around increases in pupil knowledge and understanding, but also around maintained reductions in usage over time. You can find out more about this approach online at www.kentcht.nhs.uk/just-water.

CHAPTER 7

Cannabis, NPS and Approaches to 'Illicit' Drugs

Clarifying the issues

It seems every few months the latest 'drug crisis' is reported in the media: from young people damaging their long-term mental health from cannabis use, to dicing with death from ecstasy use, via more recent stereotypes including 'spice zombies' and 'hulks on monkey dust'. Underpinning these often inaccurate stories is a wider reflection of society's views on what an illegal drug actually is, and who a 'drug user' is. Unfortunately, these views on illicit drugs and those who use them are regularly informed not by accurate statistics and population-based data, but more urban myths and sensationalist case studies. Yes, the risks around drug use are very real and a public health issue we are all involved in preventing, but extreme reporting on these issues can create drug use as something 'other' and almost 'alien'. So the person who chooses – and very rarely is this 'choice' straightforward either – to use a drug can be seen as someone outside of society, and adopting what is considered unacceptable behaviour.

If we take these representations into the classroom, credibility of information and the person delivering it becomes a real issue – mainly as some young people may be aware of friends, family members or even themselves who may have used that substance, yet not come to the extreme harms being presented. This way of delivering drug education is almost always done with the best of intentions in terms of protecting young people from those extreme risks, and is at times influenced by a perceived increase in media coverage over a certain drug which 'needs a response'. In the past it has been termed 'health terrorism' – scaring people into adopting the correct behaviour – and it is an approach without merit or evidence to support it as effective. A good case in point is mephedrone, which was one of the first drugs to be coined with the term 'legal high'. Now, that term itself was one used by the media to describe drugs which were outside of the Misuse of Drugs Act 1971 (this is essentially what categorised drugs as Class A, B or C and set out legal penalties), yet subsequently became used within policy too. We now refer to these substances as NPS (novel psychoactive substances) – partly as the Psychoactive Substances Act 2016 made them illegal, but more importantly as referring to them as 'legal' caused great confusion and increased harm associated with these drugs. According to some, these substances have been around since the 1980s (Measham *et al.*, 2010), yet only came to prominence with increased press reporting in the mid to late 2000s. This perhaps calls the 'novel' part of NPS into question, but they are certainly new to the public's consciousness.

Mephedrone (some called it Meow-meow or M-CAT) is a stimulant which acts in similar ways to drugs in that category (see Figure 7.1) in speeding up the body's central nervous system and also acting on pleasure receptors in the brain. News reports focused on deaths which were associated with mephedrone use, even though many of these were later found not to be associated with the drug. However, despite data showing that the numbers of young people using it or other NPS remained extremely low (NHS Digital, 2017), there were calls from within Parliament, communities and schools to 'tackle' it. This resulted in approaches based on the idea that delivering something is better than nothing – an approach which may be supported by moral arguments, but is also one which ultimately can do more harm than good. Similar approaches have been adopted around other NPS including synthetic cannabinoids (SCRAs) such as 'spice'. This is a substance which mimics the impact of cannabis on the brain, yet has substantially larger effects and risks and thus brings about an often unexpected and extreme experience for the user (Blackman and Bradley, 2016). It is a substance which has had greater impact on more vulnerable members of society including the homeless and offending populations, and has given rise to the very unhelpful media descriptions of 'spice zombies'. Indeed, young people themselves have expressed a distinction between those who use spice as having lower social status (Blackman and Bradley, 2016) and they are therefore less likely to use it. This goes some way to debunk the media depiction of its use being rife among certain groups of young people and adolescents.

It is worth reinforcing at this point that there should be no expectation for teachers, youth workers or other universal staff to have extensive knowledge of these substances – even drug and alcohol workers struggle to keep up! Of more importance is the willingness to look beyond the substance to the root causes of the behaviour, and to help identify the risks of adopting unhealthy coping mechanisms. This means ultimately viewing that substance use as a function of a wider unmet social or mental health need rather than an issue in and of itself. So dealing just with information about a given drug will be limited in its effectiveness in bringing about behaviour change, as the key driver for that substance use is never properly addressed.

To help put the range of drugs into context, various models such as the Drugs Wheel (Adley, 2018) give a very accurate and comprehensive depiction of a wide range of drugs according to their specific effects, legal status and risk. It is the closest thing you could get to an exhaustive list and one which is likely to be of interest to experts in the field and drug and alcohol researchers. However, for the purposes of teachers or youth workers, or even young people themselves, this can be far too detailed and unworkable at a universal level. With this in mind, Figure 7.1 uses a broad categorisation of drugs according to their effects on the central nervous system, using three umbrella categories – stimulant, depressant, hallucinogen.

- Stimulant – speeds up the nervous system

- Depressant – slows down the nervous system

- Hallucinogen – alters perceptions of the external world, visual, auditory or sensory.

There are some substances which can cross the boundaries a little. For example, dissociative drugs such as ketamine seek to separate the mind from the body to dull pain (its medical use does this in a physical sense; recreational use is more about doing this in an emotional sense). Its use as a 'horse tranquilliser' is also a bit of a myth – it has more common use as an anaesthetic, particularly in child medicine. There are also other substances such as gases (for 'sniffing' or inhaling) and nitrous oxide (laughing gas), the effects of which can be both depressant and hallucinatory depending on the dose. In many cases though, the substance will also act upon a range of pleasure receptors in the brain which give the feeling of a 'high'.

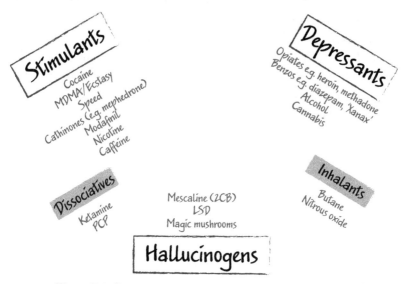

Figure 7.1: Categorising common drugs according to effects

It is also worth noting that some substances can give different effects depending on the mode of use and whether they are used with other substances. For example, cannabis is often smoked with tobacco – thus introducing a stimulant and depressant into the body. This can sometimes give young people the false impression that a drug is having one effect when it is actually doing the opposite. Alcohol is another case in point here, as it can be considered a 'bi-phasal' drug. In essence, the loss of inhibitions caused once someone starts drinking can give the impression of it being a stimulant as they are more likely to be outgoing, sociable and do things they wouldn't normally do. However, once the body starts to process the alcohol, the overall effect will be one of slowing the body down. A body map is a useful way to help young people grasp this and discuss it in a non-threatening way, and is easily adaptable to other drugs.

Approaches to education and prevention

Underpinning all attempts to prevent drug and alcohol misuse is the concept of 'first, do no harm'. This is pretty much a 'Health Promotion 101' concept – before any health-related intervention, make sure that what you do does not create more harm to that individual or group of individuals. This is where the 'something is better than nothing' approach to health education issues is deeply flawed. In many cases, delivering 'something' runs the risk of raising awareness of issues without giving enough time to actually 'learn' anything useful about them, let alone the time to develop skills related to making healthy choices around them. An obvious case from my own experience comes from supporting schools around the issue of mephedrone and other NPS in the early 2010s, before the Psychoactive Substances Act came into force in 2016. Off the back of an increase in availability and massive media coverage, schools felt a responsibility to be raising awareness of these substances as a way to prevent their use. This process raises a further secondary issue – to what extent can this knee jerk response end up raising awareness of a given drug and arguably making it seem attractive? How can that one-off session support pupils in developing skills to successfully resist or negotiate a choice to not take them or walk away? Taking an approach on NPS that 'something is better than nothing' only gives us a short time to cover the issue so we end up running the risk of raising awareness without any 'learning', turning off pupils by resorting to shock tactics rooted in urban myths, and therefore unintentionally increasing the chances of 'doing harm'. This whole process takes us back to the idea of focusing on the common skills needed to manage drug-related scenarios rather than just teaching about specific effects of a range of drugs.

Risk

This leads me to one of my main points around drug education in schools – evidence tells us it should not actually be about specific risks of specific drugs (Mentor-ADEPIS, 2017). Many successful programmes around prevention do not address individual substances per se, but wider choices around risk-taking behaviours (RisKit), specific life skills (Unplugged) or even in primary settings around self-regulation (Good Behaviour Game). Indeed, approaches to address cannabis use among pupils should be broadly similar to those adopted around mephedrone, spice or even tobacco use. In effect this is about the need for young people to practise the skills they need to negotiate real-life situations where they have choices to make around drug or alcohol use. Yes, knowledge plays a part in that, but the potential risk of taking a given drug is also made up of other things. Helping young people understand this process of assessing risk is a key skill within drug education and prevention.

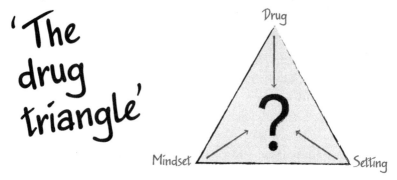

Figure 7.2: The drug triangle of risk

The so-called drug triangle shown in Figure 7.2 is a standard tool in many a drug worker's workshop toolbox. In that context, among those young people who may already be using a given substance, it is often used in support of a harm reduction approach, although it can also be used in a universal health education setting to help develop skills around assessing risk. Essentially it suggests that the risk of taking a given substance at any given time is influenced by three key factors:

1. *Drug* – this describes things to do with the drug. What is it? How much of it is there? How strong is it? Has another substance – illicit or otherwise – been used?

2. *Setting* – this describes the environment the individual is in. Are they alone? Are they with people they know? Are they indoors or outdoors? Are they somewhere they are familiar with or somewhere new?

3. *Mindset* – this describes things to do with the individual themselves. Are they feeling happy? Are they feeling anxious

or stressed or sad? Are they worried about anything? Are they tired? Do they have any medical conditions?

Taking all these things into account helps us assess the level of risk associated with a given drug – with knowledge about the drug itself playing a small part in that. It can help show that the situation a person takes a substance in is likely to be different from a previous one, as the setting or mindset is likely to be different – even if only slightly. This therefore highlights the unpredictability of drug (and alcohol) use, and the importance of helping young people understand this in helping them make healthy choices. Of course there can be further influences here such as the role and pull that forming their own identities plays in these situations, so a drug education programme which takes account of these things is likely to be more effective in giving young people the skills they need.

Use of external speakers

When talking about illegal drugs in health education, there are some understandably large barriers to teachers engaging with the topic and delivering it effectively. Seeking to address these should be a key consideration, not only for the PSHE lead within a school, but just as importantly for local public health teams. As with other topics within PSHE, a lack of training and therefore confidence in their own knowledge can cause problems:

> …we're supposed to be so-called 'experts' in all the different fields, but I know from personal experience…that a lot of teachers will kind of stick to what they're confident in, and if they're not confident, they'll avoid it or they'll just skim through it. (McKay *et al.*, 2017)

Any delivery which involves 'skimming' of the subject is likely to leave questions hanging for pupils. It is unlikely to develop skills necessary for pupils to navigate drug-related scenarios outside of school in 'real life'. Meanwhile, at the extreme end it can unwittingly normalise the very behaviours that delivery seeks to avoid. Wherever possible, standalone sessions should be minimised or at the very least planned to dovetail with other topics within a health education curriculum to minimise these risks. Where schools are delivering via drop-days or standalone sessions, the temptation is there to use external speakers who are perceived to be 'experts' in the field. This is understandable given the perception of some teachers highlighted above, yet it also brings its own pitfalls. You can often spot a range of high-profile figures promoting themselves through social media as they are looking for schools to book them to deliver talks on self-confidence, self-belief or even that catch-all term of 'resilience'. While such individuals may well have interesting things to say and this may possibly be based on first-hand experience, a key question to ask is: what actually qualifies someone to talk about mental health or drug use to young people? This is especially important to consider when we return to that idea of 'first, do no harm'.

First, there is a propensity for people (celebrity or otherwise) to endow themselves with qualifications to deliver content on PSHE and health-related topics purely on their own personal experience. Now it should be stressed that those experiences do have some place and merit, and the willingness to share those experiences is something to be applauded. However, that goodwill also has to be supported by a large element of evidence behind the approach. This takes far more than goodwill and a bit of reading up. I've had years of experience, training and personal hardship while delivering material on these topics and am still nowhere near getting it right 100 per cent of the time. Without an awareness among schools and universal services there is a risk that these well-meaning but un-evidenced offers become part of that wider approach of supporting health education and prevention in knee jerk ways via one-off sessions, drop-days or assemblies in isolation.

Second, there should be concerns about the willingness of some schools to open their doors to external speakers and end their checks at a DBS. Beyond this there needs to be better support for schools and wider education settings about what makes an evidence-based speaker, and why it is important. Recommendations from other schools and colleagues are great, but just because a speaker is energetic and engaging doesn't mean the material they deliver is up to date or utilising recognised best practice. This is where social media can have a negative role for teachers as much as pupils. You can regularly find Twitter polls on what schools look for in external speakers – reputation and recommendations are by far the most prevalent things, with little or no mention of best practice or outcome measuring. Of course to a degree strong reputations come from delivering quality work – it's more when reputations are built by doing anything rather than what is needed that we need to be careful. The blame should not really be with schools here either – it is very much a case of 'you don't know what you don't know'. Local authorities and national bodies have not done enough to help schools be aware of the need for quality assurance around PSHE and health education, and that a few simple questions can help this (my own experience in the field means I am including myself in that failing too!). Asking a few questions before booking a speaker can go a long way to finding this information out – especially around health-related content. Do they follow guidelines set out by the PSHE Association? How do they respond to the most recent guidance from Public Health England or the most recent Ofsted PSHE report? What NICE guidelines do they take into account when delivering sessions to staff or young people? With all the best will in the world, I wonder if our keen friendly celebrities can answer those questions effectively.

Let's not be naive – the root of the issue is the fact PSHE and wider health education has suffered from not being a statutory subject, so schools often are without the curriculum time or staff expertise to deliver the key life skills required to help pupils manage their wellbeing in positive ways. Greater commitment to the subject at a national strategic level should filter down to tightening up practice at a school level. If the current government consultation fulfils its promise, we should enable trained, knowledgeable staff to plan and deliver health education in evidence-based, age-appropriate ways. It should help ensure external speakers are asked the right questions about their delivery, meaning content enriches what is already being delivered in a school – not be the start and end of it.

In the UK there are examples of different quality marks for external speakers for different elements of health education, and these go some way to helping support quality external speakers. However, it will only be as good as the numbers of providers signing up to it, and ultimately the numbers of schools asking speakers if they follow evidence-based practice (the PSHE Association did some great work in the recent past with their PSHE Chartered Teacher programme). Awareness around these standards needs to be raised within local authorities and wider health professionals first. They can then support schools in what they should be looking for, and what to ask. Local health commissioners should also be sensitive to this, with many paying for groups to deliver to local schools en masse. Ultimately we need to have the needs of young people at the centre of the process, and their entitlement to receive effective and safe health education alongside the rest of the curriculum.

CHAPTER 8

Delivering Effective Mental Health and Drug Education in School

Defining what we mean by health education

A quick online search for reports and comments on mental health in schools will open up a raft of calls for better mental health or drugs 'awareness' in schools. Variations on the theme will include improved 'education' on the issues, all geared towards the prevention of the next 'crisis' young people in Britain are likely to face. A critical look at these reports, both in media outlets and professional or policy documents, will also find little detail about what those terms actually mean. There seems to be a general push that any sort of 'awareness' or 'education' will bring about improvements in mental health, without an absence of clarification on not only what we hope to achieve by this, but more importantly *how*. The importance of this is only heightened with the welcome addition of relationship and sex education (RSE) and 'health education' as part of the National Curriculum from 2020 (Department for Education, 2018). At the time of writing, the framework for health education is explicitly acknowledging the importance of how '[t]eaching on mental wellbeing is central to these subjects', with a need for 'an increased focus on risk areas such as drugs and alcohol'. While the proposed legislation is treating RSE and health education distinctly, the suggestion is that these would still be delivered within a wider framework of what we have previously known as PSHE across the UK. How that plays out in practice is key, especially if we are to go beyond the simple notion that raising awareness is all we need to deliver effective health education.

The adoption of effective evidence-based approaches to health education in schools has been historically problematic, in the main due to the non-statutory status of health education. This has resulted in the profile of the subject being secondary to those statutory elements in the wider curriculum, and most importantly wide discrepancies around not just the quality of delivery, but also the quality of support and CPD offered to staff who are delivering (Boddington, McWhirter and Stonehouse 2013; Ofsted, 2013). In the absence of any requirements for PSHE-related content within teacher training programmes, a further lack of CPD for teachers and pastoral staff has been highlighted as further reasons why PSHE as a subject was considered 'not yet good enough' by Ofsted in its subject report of 2013. The lack of updated guidance on RSE and drug education is also symptomatic of a lack of direction and support within government – the last official SRE guidance was from 2000 (when the 'S' still came before the 'R'), with the last drug education guidance published in 2004. This is all against a widening gap between health and education professionals since the abolishment of the National Healthy Schools Programme in 2010, and increases in demand for adolescent mental health support.

Evidence-based approaches

The lack of a coherent strategy around PSHE and health education has made it difficult to obtain a robust evidence base in what produces the most effective outcomes in the delivery of health education. Schools have been all coming from differing baselines in terms of delivery models, staff confidence, curriculum time, and wider whole school approaches to health and wellbeing. In many ways, this could be expected if comparing two schools from different areas in the country, but the disparity in how the subject is viewed and treated means this can often be the case in neighbouring schools from the same borough or district. We have therefore had a 'postcode lottery' (PSHE Association, 2015) around the quality of health education.

However, we are aware of correlations between schools with outstanding Ofsted judgements and outstanding models of health education delivery (Ofsted, 2013). We also know the contribution that good wellbeing makes to academic achievement for young people

(Public Health England, 2015). The root of this can be the model of delivery schools have historically adopted for delivering health education which broadly fall into one of three categories:

1. Delivery via off-curriculum days or 'drop-days'

2. Delivery through weekly tutor time

3. Dedicated curriculum time.

On the face of it, this model is understandably appealing. Finding curriculum time for a non-statutory subject is very difficult for school leaders, so dedicating just one or two days a year to a topic can be seen as a viable alternative. These days are normally organised by each school year rather than the whole school, and delivered through a carousel model with each class receiving one lesson on a range of topics over the course of the day – so a six-period school day would give time for six different lessons to be delivered. Schools may be able to use some external services to support this – some offering services free of charge, and some for a fee.

Some of the pitfalls of delivering via this route are how pupils are likely to respond to this. At times, levels of engagement drop as they are aware that this is not a 'normal' school day, to the extent that attendance on those days drops too – with those more vulnerable pupils who would benefit most from the topics more likely to vote with their feet. Without any other delivery on those topics throughout the curriculum, this model also runs the risk of raising awareness and intrigue among pupils without giving the time to explore the issues effectively and embed learning. In many ways the 'something is better than nothing' adage may not apply (McDonald and Tomlin, 2017), with the opposite being the case if content is not handled effectively. It is for these reasons that this model of delivery is widely considered least effective (Mentor-ADEPIS, 2017; PSHE Association, 2017; Ofsted, 2013) and not meeting the needs of pupils. It is not uncommon for schools who deliver via the drop-day model to point to pupil feedback which is positive about these days and shows that pupils appreciate having them. That feedback is then used to justify the continuation of this model. However, for these schools, pupil baseline is often having no health education at all – so they are more likely to respond positively to having something delivered to them even if it does not follow best practice. A perhaps crude analogy would be that one or two sports days in isolation per year would not make a PE curriculum, so why should we use this model for PSHE? It is worth noting, however, that these days can have benefit when they are delivered in addition to a spiral curriculum.

Alternatively, some schools may choose to deliver their health education through weekly 'tutor time' slots, where pupils have contact time with their nominated tutor who has responsibility for pastoral and wider non-subject specific issues which impact on pupils in their tutor group. This is often seen as an easy way to slot the topic into a regular curriculum-style model without taking up extra time on the timetable. It also ensures schools can have some level of spiral planning built into planning and delivery so content is built on year on year. These are things which reflect good practice so on the face of it are very valid reasons for adopting this approach.

The flip side, though, is that tutor time is reserved not just for delivery of health education topics, but for wider pastoral and school management functions. This means delivery of a given topic at a nominated point in the school calendar is subject to other wider school issues which may take precedence. This model also requires all tutors in a school to be confident and competent in delivering the lesson content which in some cases is highly unlikely to be achieved due to pressures on CPD time. This would require all teaching staff to have access to training on all topics covered by a PSHE or health education curriculum. A tutor who has not received CPD on a given topic is therefore an unconfident one. This means lessons are either not delivered at all, or delivered 'to the resource' – that means it is not responsive to the needs of the group and is less likely to be interactive and meaningful. All these things are entirely understandable and a function of the system teachers operate in rather than the teachers themselves. Ultimately, though, we still end up with inconsistent delivery and outcomes from health education. A further downside of the tutor time model is in those schools who operate vertical tutor systems. In these schools, tutor groups are not made up of 30 pupils in a single year group, but by five or six pupils from five different year groups. While this has some benefits in terms of pupils building relationships and responsibilities towards those of different ages, it makes delivery of PSHE and health education problematic. What is suitable and relevant content for pupils at 15 is not relevant or suitable for pupils at age 11. So the potential for outcomes to be minimised or even harmful for some is increased.

The most effective and desirable model of delivery is via dedicated curriculum time utilising teams of specialist teachers (Mentor-ADEPIS, 2017; PSHE Association, 2017 ; Ofsted, 2013). A smaller dedicated team of staff makes CPD delivery more manageable and effective. It makes the planning process easier and more collaborative, and results in improved satisfaction and outcomes from both teachers and pupils alike. In the main, these teachers will still have their dedicated subject to deliver, but will also have health education teaching time built into their personal timetables. The resulting increased satisfaction and confidence also points towards greater consistency in keeping the team together and ultimately a better standard of delivery. There are those who propose that these specialist teams are made up of expert, external professionals in the given topic which is being covered. While the use of these external speakers to enrich what is already being delivered definitely has its benefits, being the sole deliverer of health education does have its downfalls, most notably, that their expertise is not in teaching pedagogy, nor are they aware of the specific needs and dynamics of a given class group. This therefore minimises the effectiveness of delivery and can also impact on the safe environment needed to discuss and explore some of the key issues covered throughout this book.

Delivery of mental health education

When it comes to actually *delivering* any material around mental health and drug education, there are some key things to consider. One of these is how we frame mental health in particular, and the types of language we adopt when talking about it. We have seen some progress in how the media report mental health issues, but we also still see regular links being made between mental illness and serious crime. We still see regular use of the so-called 'head clutcher' stock photo alongside mental health stories and articles. This represents a very negative image of mental health rooted in despair, hopelessness, struggle and suffering. We still see ill-informed documentaries on depression which can also do more harm than good (particularly when shown to young people in an unsupportive learning environment). Conversely, we also need to recognise the positive work in challenging stigma in the UK which has been done by the likes of the Time to Change campaign, Mind and Young Minds to name a few. This has resulted in us talking more about mental health. However, against this wider societal backdrop, we do still need to think seriously about how we frame mental health for young people and get positive messages across.

One example to consider is how we talk about conditions and emotions like depression, anxiety and stress. Generally, we hear professionals, the media and even politicians refer to pupils who 'have' anxiety, or who 'suffer' from stress, depression or other conditions related to poor mental health. As we have explored already, some of these terms are used to describe varying states of mental wellbeing from temporary dips in mood to longer-lasting mental illness which severely impact on an individual's daily functioning. Immediately this tends to clinicalise what those young people – or staff – are feeling which can cause issues for two reasons. First, it immediately supposes these pupils *need* a clinical response. Like Stan Kutcher (2017) suggests, this can mean clinicalising everyday experiences. These clinical responses can mean either school-based counselling services, or referral on to wider CAMHS interventions, often meaning a long waiting list for assessment. While many young people do require a clinical intervention, not all young people experiencing these symptoms need this. Second, and with greater relevance to delivering mental health education, there is a risk of almost conditioning pupils into thinking that these things are to be avoided. This means that if a young person experiences anxiety or stress then they can feel they have 'got it' and there's no way out. Not only that, but if they have 'got it' and it is something they have been told they need to avoid, they can feel they can't let anyone know what they are feeling as it means they have failed in some way. In both examples, this simple trick of language can deskill those staff within the school environment who have the potential to develop skills in pupils to manage these instances – either as pastoral teams or through a well-programmed curriculum of health education – as it shuts down conversation. It makes it difficult to explore what has caused those feelings of stress or anxiety, what they actually 'feel' like, and most importantly what someone can do to restore good mental health and feel better.

So it is here that we can make a clear distinction between when we are *experiencing* feelings and emotions like anxiety, and when we are *suffering* from them. This may seem a little petty, but we should consider how this simple shift in thinking and contextualising of mental health in schools can impact on whole school approaches to wellbeing. This helps us normalise rather than medicalise elements of everyday life (Kutcher, 2017). It also opens up the opportunities to discuss and explore those causes and healthy ways of coping, and also to help young people develop a shared language around mental health. Importantly, it supports that proactive approach to promoting positive mental health rather than the reactive one of avoiding poor mental health. We need to remember our mental health exists on a continuum, and it is totally expected and 'normal' that we move along that continuum throughout our day. There are things that are likely to cause us to worry, to feel a little anxious, or to feel a bit stressed. There are also things that will bring us relief, to help us feel relaxed, or feel happy. It is only through experiencing the negative side of the continuum that we can recognise what causes us to feel anxious or stressed, and more importantly what we can do to manage that and move us back to the positive end of that continuum. Exams *are* going to cause someone to feel stressed. Transitions of any description *are* likely to cause someone to feel anxious. New situations may also do the same. We need to acknowledge that these are all totally understandable and quite normal reactions to different situations. But if we only refer to people 'suffering' from these feelings, it limits our ability to recognise what these feelings are, what causes them, and then most importantly how to respond positively to them. It means we are more likely to refer pupils on to specialist services when actually they need the time and space to explore how to restore positive mental health themselves.

Part of this should also be around helping pupils develop effective language around their mental health and wellbeing. This includes identifying brief experiences of low or good mood as well as when things feel like they could be getting worse. Finding ways to effectively express how they feel is really important here; using creative tools to do so when talking about them can be difficult. This includes artwork, modelling, or creative writing such as lyrics or poetry (Chapter 9 has more detailed examples of some of these). These things can also serve a purpose as positive coping strategies to restore good mental health when needed. However, promoting these as things to do in a reactive sense, after it is needed, is a bit like chasing our own tails. This is where health education should incorporate these tools, with focused time for pupils to practise them so they are able to use them when needed to prevent *experiences* of poor mental health becoming clinical issues when they have no idea of how to manage them.

So the question then becomes: do current models of health education allow that time for young people to develop these skills and a 'language' of mental health? There are some who would question whether that is something for schools or parents to do. Adopting a view that it is parental responsibility alone does not conform to the duty for schools to promote pupil wellbeing, nor does it meet the needs of those pupils who don't have the positive relationships at home for those skills to be developed and nurtured there. Now this shouldn't take away the need for clinical responses for those pupils (and staff) who are suffering from frequent bouts of anxiety, or more extreme bouts either, but it does require us to think a little about how sporadic *experiences* of anxiety should not automatically equal a mental illness needing a clinical response.

This whole process isn't helped by ministerial speeches on youth mental health constantly referring to the numbers 'suffering' from anxiety, stress or depression. Neither is it helpful when research on youth mental health is also reported in the same way. Quite often what is reported as 'numbers of pupils suffering from anxiety' is actually either self-reported by pupils themselves without any qualifying of what 'suffering' means, or questions which ask about experiencing anxiety being reported as them suffering from it (Kutcher, 2017). Again, this feeds that wider discourse about these feelings being something we should shield young people from. Yet if we are shielding them from these feelings, how are they supposed to learn how to recognise what causes them, let alone how to deal with it? The worst case scenario is that the first time they experience stronger feelings of stress or anxiety are when they are about to sit a GCSE or A-level. It's no wonder then, when these feelings get out of control. Focusing on these skills and tools then becomes a more meaningful use of health education than simple 'mental health awareness' dealing only with facts and extreme consequences or poor mental health and mental illness. Perhaps more importantly, these skills can then represent more acceptable and confidence-building content, which teachers feel more comfortable delivering. This last point is exemplified in the passion that well-trained and supported teachers of PSHE and health education have for the subject – even considering they have their own specialist subjects they were trained in.

Personal disclosures

In general curriculum subjects, class teachers could be said to hold 'expert' and at times 'coercive' forms of power on account of their own training, expert knowledge, choice of content for a given lesson, and the ability to apply a reprimand for anyone breaking rules. Ideally we would want to be exhibiting more 'referent' power (as many already do) where classroom roles are based on mutual respect and identification of the teacher as a leader of the class. In many ways the promotion of involving young people in the development of a PSHE and health education curriculum is therefore disrupting these traditional concepts of power, by creating a more balanced state of 'expert' power between teacher and pupils, whereas the teacher normally holds all the cards in terms of knowledge, expertise and assessment. Traditional health education topics are arguably more open to pupil acquisition of knowledge independently of school than other curriculum subjects, which will naturally impact on this shift in expert power. Particularly where there is a common identified lack of support for delivery staff (Ofsted, 2013), this has the potential to be wrongly perceived as tipping the balance in the opposite direction with pupils holding more expert power, resulting in a more one-sided and coercive teaching dynamic to compensate – effectively the feeling of 'but they know more than me!' It has to be said that in many cases this is not the case, as has been discussed already in terms of the misperceptions young people and adults have from media and other unreliable sources of information on drug use in particular. Therefore, we end up with the more important focus of the teacher of health education being one of *facilitator* for applying the skills needed to use and negotiate this acquired knowledge in real-life scenarios. This is where lessons can become a more health-promoting process, empowering pupils to be self-sufficient in managing their own health choices and behaviours. This process cements the importance of developing ground rules as part of any effective approach to PSHE and health education.

ACTIVITY

Using the PSHE Association's ground rules as a starting point, encourage young people to discuss what would help make a 'safe' environment to explore different health issues. Graffiti sheets can be placed around the room for them to share their ideas in a practical way, and can then be brought back together to summarise and agree on them. This results in an agreed way of managing questions, potential disclosures and the need to keep things 'in the room' – effectively not going outside the classroom and gossiping about any personal experiences which have been brought up in the session. This also gives the opportunity for staff to remind young people of safeguarding procedures in a more supportive context.

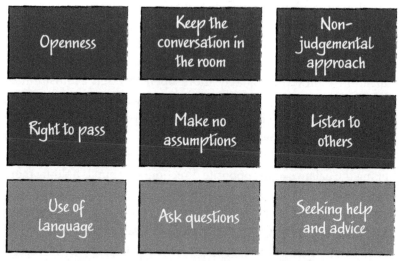

Figure 8.1: PSHE Association's ground rules for PSHE

My personal background in drug and alcohol work has helped me tread the imaginary line of disclosing personal experiences with extreme caution. Indeed, this experience was very much following a mantra of 'don't do it'. This view has evidence to back it up, where the use of ex-users in schools who talk openly about their own experience and substance-using history has had adverse impact on pupil outcomes (Mentor-ADEPIS, 2017). There are some examples to the contrary, it must be said, although the reliability of these evaluations is at times unclear. Within a drug and alcohol education context, a common question from the floor can be 'do you puff then, sir?' (referring to cannabis). A general response can be along the lines of 'I don't really think that matters – I think it's more important that I have experience of listening to and reading about experiences of young people from different backgrounds. Learning from their experiences is more important and gives me more to offer you.' That said, we do need to appreciate where they are often coming from here – they are generally wanting that teacher to clarify their authority to talk to them about a subject many other adults in their lives feel either unable or too uncomfortable to talk about. I always felt having that standard response and experiences to fall back on contributed to that authority though. Ultimately it didn't follow their school experiences of an unsupported and untrained teacher going red with embarrassment at the thought of answering them.

ACTIVITY

To help support staff delivering drug education, give an opportunity for teachers to share some awkward questions they are worried about hearing from pupils, and share possible answers to maintain that distance and safe environment. This can be done as part of a staff meeting or by using graffiti sheets in a staff room over the course of a week. Giving the opportunity for staff to learn from each other about how to manage these awkward questions can be an empowering and confidence-building process. Some examples are highlighted in Table 8.1.

Table 8.1: Answering awkward questions from young people

Awkward questions from young people	Possible response
Do you do drugs, then?	That would mean talking from just one person's experience. I think the knowledge I have got from going on training and talking to young people means I have experiences from lots of young people to draw on – that is more important.

cont.

Awkward questions from young people	Possible response
What do you know about SCRAs? (This could take the form of any substance you may not know about.)	That's not something I am aware of, although you could be using a different term than I am used to. We can find out more about it together after today's lesson if you like.
That just doesn't happen!	We all have different experiences of different behaviours. What we have looked at is one possible consequence of [drug use, mental illness, etc.]
My mum smokes cannabis for pain relief. (This is becoming more likely with increased awareness around medical benefits of some illicit drugs.)	At the moment cannabis is still illegal in the UK. Some medications are derived from drugs like cannabis, but the contents are strictly controlled and the medicine prescribed by a doctor. Someone growing and smoking their own cannabis is still breaking the law.

This last question needs careful and sensitive handling as a young person in that situation may become distressed at the thought of a parent or other relative breaking the law in this way. Cannabis-derived medicines generally do not contain the psychoactive ingredient which gets people 'stoned', and instead only contains the ingredient which can provide pain relief for certain conditions. So-called 'homegrown' cannabis will still contain the psychoactive element, making it illegal.

Distancing

These elements can be used to inform a default position on 'distancing techniques' in PSHE and health education – that is, keeping a distance by not disclosing personal information, leaving thorough planning and facilitating skills to get that authority across. This approach has strong links with the social norms approach which was explored in Chapter 4. To summarise, a social norm, or 'normative', approach seeks to challenge pupil misperceptions on influential peer behaviour by promoting the positive choices we want young people to adopt, over the unhealthy ones we want to avoid. With this in mind, using personal disclosure can unwittingly normalise the very behaviours we want to protect against. Regardless of the overall message you are trying to convey, the over-riding one can be 'Sir has done that and he turned out all right, so maybe it's OK for me to do it too'. This is a common pitfall for some when delivering drug education, and is understandable where teachers may be expected to undertake delivery without any prior training.

In contrast, the field of mental health education has more examples of individuals using personal disclosure. Here there seems to be more support for a degree of personal disclosure as a way of bringing authenticity to the work and the messages we convey. On the surface of it, we can be forgiven for thinking this helps break the stigma around the topic with the previous example around drug education being turned into something more positive – 'Sir has recovered from his mental health issues, so why can't I…?' The problem is: how a message is intended to be delivered by someone is not always how it is received. That is where the fine line lies between intention and reception and there are risks for those who choose to walk that line, making it more difficult to ensure that that session really can 'first, do no harm'.

In spite of this, we can explore the difference in training adults compared to educating young people. It is here where personal disclosures can be far more palatable, but is this coming from a point of furthering practice or is it just less problematic than doing it with young people? There are numerous examples of hearing inspirational people talk about their personal experiences, and their journey to recovery. My own experiences of listening to Pooky Knightsmith on many occasions has also prompted discussion on this, posing the question that if we were talking about cancer would we be so sheepish around personal disclosure in that realm? Either way, the support for personal disclosure is seen by many as a valid way to challenge stigma, and to have a very prevalent example of that 'in the room'. Time to Change and other campaigns regularly use personal stories as a way of challenging stigma around mental ill health. These can be in the form of blogs, posters, video clips and audio clips for radio. These resources have the desired impact of challenging stigma and getting people talking about mental health who wouldn't have done so before – and this really is great. Ultimately though, if these stories are out there already through these avenues, do we need personal disclosure on the part of teachers anyway? A key concern here is that we don't jump in with both feet and start disclosing in unsafe ways for both the adult and young people involved. What we do need to consider, though, is the place for talking about positive experiences of accessing support and of recovery. In this way, we are normalising the process of gaining support and breaking down stigma around that, rather than of mental illness in and of itself. Again, this returns us to the need to adopt a life skills approach within PSHE and health education by supporting young people to develop the confidence and skills to access such support – including substance use, mental health, sexual health and general GP services.

Harm reduction versus 'Just Say No'

Switching our focus to drug and alcohol education specifically, we can sometimes fall into a binary approach of either the 'Just Say No' approach, or one around 'harm reduction'. The former has already been tackled in this book as an ineffective way of planning and delivering drug education, while the latter is an approach taken by young people's drug services around helping young people reduce the harm associated with drug use. It is also one mistakenly assumed to be about 'telling them how to do it safely', when it is in fact aimed at reducing the likelihood of harm coming to those *who may already be using*. In many ways, drug education, as part of wider universal health education, needs to sit somewhere between the two.

What can sometimes make a consistency of approach difficult are media stories about young people coming to harm or fatal consequences as a result of drug use, normally around summer festival season. Are these tragedies as simple as a dodgy batch of ecstasy, a lack of quality drug education in local schools, wider social determinants, or a combination of all the above? The media will often put it down to the 'rogue batch' or a lazy nod towards pills all of a sudden being marketed at children through being stamped with images relating to the latest craze in youth subcultures – a view which is commonly debunked. At times, and to an extent rightly so, we do put this down to a combination of the wider determinants of health discussed in Chapter 3. My only issue with this is that it can wash over things we can learn in respect to the responses discussed, focusing on too much of a structural influence rather than the individual choices and skills we can be developing in young people at the same time.

In light of the occasions where young teenagers are involved in these incidents, we perhaps need to think more about not just the presence and quality of drug education, but again about *how* it is delivered. In particular, this comes on the back of understandable calls from youth services and drug workers for more harm reduction delivery in schools. In principle this seems like a reasonable and progressive response, but there should arguably also be consideration given to the principles of Fraser Guidelines here. By this I mean rather than capacity to consent to medical intervention in a clinical sense, we should be thinking about the capacity of young people to make distinctions between harm reduction and general information on drug use. I probably need to be clear that as an ex drug worker who has delivered hours of harm reduction in the past I am 100 per cent behind harm reduction for those groups deemed at risk or vulnerable to drug use. Indeed, the success of early intervention programmes are starting to give us great evidence to support approaches which identify young people with a tendency to develop risk-taking behaviours in the future (the Centre for Analysis of Youth Transitions has many examples of these programmes). What are really important when considering any drug education which includes direct harm reduction messages are the unintended consequences of delivering these elements at a universal level – for example, to all young people in a year group – and whether we could be inadvertently normalising use by doing so. Some evidence (Mentor-ADEPIS, 2013a) does suggest that there could be benefit in this around alcohol education specifically, and with older age groups, but I'm still not sure about wider substances with lower population use in these age groups as shown by national datasets discussed in earlier chapters.

As well as questions from young people themselves, a school or youth setting embarking on a programme of drug and alcohol education can also elicit questions and suggestions from adults within the school community – these could be teachers, school leaders, parents, governors or others with vested community interest. While these comments can often have the best interests of the community at heart, we need to be prepared to challenge those which do not follow evidence-based practice. Some suggestions on how these can be sensitively challenged are given in Table 8.2.

Table 8.2: Answering awkward questions
from the wider school community

Awkward questions from adults within the school community	Possible response
Drugs are dangerous. Why not just tell them not to do it?	Telling a teenager not to do something often results in them doing that same thing! Accepted best practice is to focus on the skills young people need to navigate real-life situations rather than just saying no.
If we tell them too much they are likely to start using drugs!	The evidence we have tells us that is not the case. Young people are highly likely to come into drug or alcohol-related situations outside of school so we need to give them the skills to protect themselves rather than ignoring the issues. Parents, teachers and young people themselves want these issues covered in school.
Bring in sniffer dogs.	This is not recognised best practice and is against both official DfE and police guidance. Sniffer dogs are more likely to create distrust between pupils and school, meaning pupils are highly unlikely to engage in health education or ask for support when they need it.
We need to have a zero tolerance approach to all drug and alcohol incidents.	The reasons for a young person using drugs or alcohol are often complex and a result of other unmet needs. Taking a zero tolerance approach and excluding young people exposes them to greater vulnerability and can make their circumstances worse.

Lots of well-meaning educators in schools and non-formal settings can respond to specific incidents, perhaps influenced by community responses too, by switching their drug education delivery to harm reduction methods. That is fair enough where local data and intelligence tells a school that a significant number of young people in a peer group are using or are likely to use. However, for those younger Key Stage 3 pupils, for example, we need to consider the extent to which a blanket harm reduction response reinforces the misperception that this is something the majority of their peers are doing, and how this can negatively impact their own choices around substance use. As such, more thought and research is needed to explore the normative impacts on young people's behaviour of harm reduction approaches in universal settings. My suspicion is that inclusion of harm reduction sessions in some schools would be at the expense of other drug education provision a school currently has planned. Therefore the risk is that harm reduction becomes the only drug education these young people receive. While the information would be undoubtedly of use to some young people in a given group, this would also reinforce the negative normalising of the unwanted behaviour for others – especially where the general information and essential skill development would be missing.

So we need to be wary of the knee jerk response which has often been adopted to drug-related incidents such as these. Regardless of the substance, we are still stuck in a general idea of throwing information at young people in the hope that some of it sticks. While many PSHE leads and local authorities are working more progressively in their curriculum and working towards the life skills approach, we do need to be wary about the wider community responses which are often mis-informed by poor media reporting on these issues.

POINTS FOR PRACTICE

Mike Armiger supports schools and other organisations around developing supportive and appropriate responses to mental illness in children and young people. When it comes to thinking about how we talk about mental health, he has these tips:

1. Encourage curiosity around emotions. Too often we ask children to tell us how they are feeling. We ask them to pick an emotion so we can move on and we hope that it will help them rationalise and process. We don't feel emotions singularly; you can feel nervous whilst feeling angry, sad and all of the other emotions we talk with children about. When you ask a child how they're feeling, if they come back with an emotion ask them 'what else?' This way they get used to articulating a few. Let's talk about emotional states not singular emotions. If they can't articulate it there and then ask them to come back in a few days and let you know if they can. We should not rush young people towards cognitive labels, especially when we consider the complexities of emotion and neurobiology.

2. Words matter. Our language has more influence than we know. It passes through generations, so as understanding evolves, so must our words. It is useful to separate mental health and acute needs so we avoid pathologising too quickly. When you ask people what they think when you say the words 'mental health', regularly they come back with 'depression, anxiety, bipolar', etc. Those are acute needs. Mental health according to the World Health Organization is defined as a state of wellbeing, so humanising the language around mental health is important.

Instead let's use terms like 'low mood', 'saturation', 'overwhelm', 'distress'.

Using these terms will help remind everyone that we are all human and have a brain. This would also encourage staff in their conversations with pupils instead of feeling fear when they hear the term 'mental health'.

3. Suicide (and self-harm) is one of those things we don't talk about, mainly because it's a scary thought and also a complex subject. But if you're going to talk about it, which I hope you will, here are a few tips:

    i.   You don't have to be mentally ill to make an attempt on your life or self-harm. People are in overwhelming amounts of distress and often for good reason. People tragically sometimes see it as the only way out or the only way to regulate their distress.

    ii. Suicide was de-criminalised in 1961 and referring to 'committing suicide' meant that you were referring to a crime being committed. Completed or successful/ unsuccessful suicide links success and failure to suicide and I don't know about you, but I find it a rather odd thing to do. So if you are going to talk about suicide, let's say 'died by suicide', 'took their own life' or 'made an attempt on their life'.

    iii. Safety plans are a brilliant tool for anyone experiencing overwhelming distress. These are often used with people who experience harmful thoughts and ideation.

Essentially it is about planning for 'what happens next time' and helping someone identify what they can do to stay safe. You don't have to be a clinician to use this tool either. Anyone can help someone using this tool.

4. Use the word 'hope'. Hope is something many have a strange relationship with. Often we feel it's missing. And in the depths of some people's distress, they can often find hope and a sense of a future difficult to imagine and consider. However, do remember this is not relentless positivity without validating someone's feelings. 'Yeah, that must suck', 'Yeah, I get it', 'That must be challenging then. How can we/what can we/the future', 'Here's something I do to remember hope.' These are all good phrases to use. A sense of the future and of hope is something we all need.

5. Talk about vulnerability. If someone had told me very simply that it is possible for the brain to convince an individual of things that aren't true, or feed into a false narrative, I would have jumped up and hugged them. I thought it was just me. These aren't voices; they're self-doubt, vulnerabilities, insecurities, etc. If we encouraged our students to talk about vulnerability, I bet we wouldn't be signposting more young people to anger management and other interventions that don't come back to the vulnerability someone is experiencing. We would also discover many more barriers to learning and growth that we could support. Talking about vulnerability is uncomfortable but it is also full of truth and courage and ultimately it's liberating to know others can feel the same way. We need to get away from the message that you have to be a trained counsellor to discuss these things in this context. You don't. You just need to be a human being.

Mike can be found on Twitter @MikeArmiger.

CHAPTER 9

Developing Healthy and Positive Coping

In addition to the issue-specific approaches already covered around both the prevention and support of young people around mental health and substance use, this chapter seeks to provide some simple ideas for coping mechanisms which can be suggested to those who are struggling. Indeed, while this book is aimed at supporting young people, many examples are just as useful for adults. The examples suggested here have formed the core of my own personal work for the past 20 years and as such are an amalgamation of therapeutic approaches, combined with elements of youth work practice, all combined with things I have stumbled on and adapted from other great practitioners I have had the privilege of learning from.

Offering a listening, non-judgemental ear

At a base level, young people who are struggling with their mental health, and perhaps coping in unhealthy ways, are looking for someone to stop and listen to them.

> It's this communication that actually, everything that is going on inside me is really ugly, or is really scary, but I'm going to show you that in this sort of wound or this cut, and if you react badly to what you see on the outside then I'm not gonna show you what's on the inside. 'Cause that's the really scary thing. (Young person, taken from *No Harm Done* film for professionals, 2016)

As a practitioner in school, youth or health settings, our time is precious. We are also subject to managing our own wellbeing in the workplace, and the pressures we feel can make it difficult sometimes to offer that listening ear – especially if we are aware that another pupil or young person is also in need of our time and attention. However, young people tell us that one of the most important things we can do is to just sit, and listen. If only they knew how difficult that can be! Some suggestions for helping that process are highlighted in Figure 9.1, with some explanations following it.

Figure 9.1: Supporting those difficult 'listening' conversations

Invariably, young people will first test the water and ask for our time at the most inconvenient moment. Just before the end of lunch break, as we are leaving for the day or for another meeting, or when we are passing in a corridor. Why do they choose those moments? Because the risk of rejection is incredibly low. If that professional doesn't have the time, then it is easy to blame it on other pressures. But when we are caught in those moments, it is more important to offer that time further down the line – 'I can't talk to you now but come back in an hour when I can give you my full attention.'

Even when we do give them our full attention, how often do we just 'listen'? It is not about finding immediate solutions to what is presented to us – that isn't a realistic expectation if a young person has been struggling for a while. Most importantly, they don't expect us to wave a magic wand in these moments, just be able to start that process of finding out what support works for them. One of the most difficult things is to 'embrace the silence'. It is perhaps the most defining piece of advice I have had from working with Pooky Knightsmith in recent years, and also one of the most difficult things to do. We need to let young people find their own voice and use their own words to explain their feelings and emotions rather than saying 'yes' or 'no' to our well-intentioned but sometimes rushed suggestions. So embrace that silence, let it breathe, and support that young person to say what they truly need to. If we need to help, sticking to open questions ensures they are still in control of the conversation.

We also need to show we are listening by how we frame our responses. At the core of this is to recognise why most people work with young people in the first place – to educate, support and help them live healthy lives to their full potential. So if a young person is talking about how they feel inadequate, fat, lonely and no good at school – what is our gut response? Think about that for a moment… If we are honest, our reactions are well-meaning and would generally fall along the lines of 'no, you're not fat', 'you have loads of friends', 'you're really clever and are doing great at school'. We understandably want to reassure and help them feel better about themselves. But in the moment of them disclosing those difficult feelings to us, after weeks of building up to it, what do those responses say? However much we may not agree with what has been said, those responses say we haven't really listened to them. So however difficult it is, we need to *show* we are listening by acknowledging those difficult feelings they are describing, but we can still give that hope that together we can find ways to feel better. This harks back in part to 'the 3Ps' highlighted in Chapter 3 around safe policies, safe people and safe places. Keeping these ideals at the front of our minds can help us focus on what is important 'in that moment' for a young person reaching out for a listening ear.

> I felt the weight of responsibility to get it right and have all the answers… I wanted to put everything right for her and make everything OK, and I realised that wasn't actually what she needed at that point, she just needed to be listened to. (Teacher, taken from *No Harm Done* film for professionals, 2016)

To help manage the awkwardness of that whole process, we can find ways to reduce the intensity of the conversation, while still prioritising the needs of the individual. Some ways to help this are:

- Walking and talking

- Distraction tools – see section on 'colouring' below!

- Distancing language – giving examples of 'young people' in general rather than focusing on the individual.

A key thing to remember is what that young person may be going through while they are talking to you. Especially in relation to unhealthy coping behaviours like self-harm or drug and alcohol use, a young person is likely to be experiencing feelings of shame and heightened anxiety. Reinforcing the support which they are able to access, either through school pastoral teams or external services, can help with some of these feelings by offering some hope and positive outcomes which they can now look towards. The fear and anxiety of family members finding out, or social care becoming involved, is also a very real concern for some young people. For many, this delays reaching out for support too. Again, staying positive and hopeful about the future can help dampen these worries, while also being realistic about school safeguarding processes.

Colouring

I have been quick to admit it in the past – I was the world's biggest cynic when adult colouring became a 'thing' in this country. I thought it would be a fad which would run out of steam as quickly as it gained traction. I have since come to appreciate how powerful this simple strategy can be for young people and adults to manage overwhelming feelings. It means being able to get absorbed in something which has a definable start and end, something which can be quite sensory in terms of going from black and white to full of colour, and most importantly something which can wholly distract us from whatever it is that is causing distress. There are some great resources out there including Pooky Knightsmith's *The Healthy Coping Colouring Book and Journal* (2016), but a simple print-out from the web can be just as useful. I have worked with schools and colleges who themselves have been surprised by the take-up of these activities. One college in particular, which by its very nature had a high number of vulnerable 16–18-year-olds on roll, expressed how its wellbeing suite couldn't keep up with the demand for colouring sheets. There were swathes of students who would walk round the college site full of bravado and bolshiness, who still needed ten minutes a day to themselves to sit, be quiet, and manage the stresses they came across both in and outside of college life. As has already been highlighted, we need to recognise the preventative impact this has not just on traditional notions of poor mental health such as self-harm, but also wider risky behaviours and drug and alcohol use.

Art

The role of creative activities is also of benefit to young people who are struggling with their mental health. This isn't just about painting, but involves more tactile activities too such as modelling with clay, plasticine or even LEGO®. LEGO® therapy has enjoyed a lot of traction within primary education in particular (LeGoff et al., 2014), and plasticine modelling, as a way of young people expressing in a creative way what they cannot seem to put into words, has immense benefit. Addaction's Mind and Body programme has these activities at its core when supporting young people to develop healthy coping and self-soothing skills, with participants continuing to utilise these skills to cope in healthy ways once the programme had finished (Still, 2017).

Writing and drawing

In a similar way to the creative and distractive process of art described above, young people can find it easier to write about their feelings as it removes some of the barriers put up by having to talk to an adult in a one-to-one scenario, especially if a 'walk and talk' session isn't feasible. Some young people will use this writing process as a further coping strategy at home or other settings, and this can take the form of a journal, a simple account of their experiences, or something more creative like a story, poetry or even song lyrics. For some, drawing what they are feeling can also be useful. This is effectively a way of encouraging young people to find a way to get out of their heads and onto paper what is causing them worry and discomfort.

Symbolically, being encouraged and able to do that shows them that those thoughts and worries are no longer inside their head, guiding their thoughts and feelings. This invariably makes those thoughts seem less daunting, threatening or worthy of poring over. Some young people like to demonstrate this further by screwing up the piece of paper once they are finished with it!

Games

In the spirit of disrupting the dreaded one-to-one scenario which can cause many adults, let alone young people, to clam up, finding interactive and simple games to use can be effective. One from my old days as a drug worker is the use of a wooden tower game. To help young people to explore how they and others can experience negative and positive emotions, and find positive ways to cope with them, prompting questions can be written on the side of each wooden block. As the game is played and blocks are removed from the tower and placed back on top, the corresponding question can be read out to stimulate discussion. In a group setting, that question can be opened out to all the group. This is particularly effective when exploring 'what works' for coping as it helps young people to hear from their peers about what strategies they find useful – thus increasing their power and the likelihood of trying them. It can reinforce the idea that 'it's not just me' who experiences these feelings, while also helping develop a language around hope as Mike Armiger suggested in Chapter 8. This also follows Rick Bradley's suggestions in Chapter 5 around young people learning from each other's experiences in safe and distanced ways. Where possible, try to give ownership to the young people you are working with by getting them to write the prompting statements and questions on the blocks. Again, this helps with positive engagement with the activity.

Figure 9.2: Developing a wooden tower game as a supportive conversation tool

For younger children, discussions can be supported through the use of card games. One I have found useful is an adaptation of the traditional 'Happy Families' card game. Rather than having nuclear families – mum, dad, brother and sister – which rarely represent the make-up of families today, this includes a range of different families including single parent, same-sex parents, grandparents, pets, and those with a range of disabilities. This helps children explore how their families are all different and reinforce the fact that 'it's not just me'. It can also help them explore what different stresses and pressures there can be on their peers, as well as how we can help them feel better.

Figure 9.3: Fabulous families: a card game for children

You can find a PDF of this card game at https://ianmacpshe.blogspot. com/2019/03/fabulous-families-resource.html.

These are just a few simple and accessible suggestions to help develop healthy coping strategies. The key is giving young people opportunities to practise them before they are needed – as stressed in earlier chapters, this means focusing on skills rather than just knowledge. Additionally, we need to recognise that these strategies are personal to all of us, so the more opportunities we give to talk about them and share experiences the better. A key thing to take away from this book as a whole is that need to share practice among other professionals, while also encouraging young people and families to do the same.

APPENDIX

Organisations Producing Materials and Resources for Working with Children and Young People on Mental Health and Drug Use

PSHE Association: www.pshe-association.org.uk – resources, training and toolkits around all PSHE and health education topics.

Charlie Waller Memorial Trust: www.cwmt.org.uk – resources, training and online webinars around mental health.

Mentor-ADEPIS: www.mentor-adepis.org – resources, toolkits and briefing papers around alcohol and drug education.

Time to Change: www.time-to-change.org.uk – resources, training and campaign materials challenging mental health stigma.

Young Minds: www.youngminds.org.uk – resources and training around youth mental health.

Boingboing Resilience Forum: www.boingboing.org.uk – toolkits and resources focusing on building resilience in schools and communities.

Dove Self-Esteem Project: www.dove.com/uk/dove-self-esteem-project.html – online toolkits and resources around self-esteem.

Rise Above: www.riseabove.org.uk – online platform for videos and vlogs on health and lifestyle topics for young people. Associated Rise Above Schools site hosts classroom resources for PSHE and health education: https://campaignresources. phe.gov.uk/schools/topics/rise-above/overview.

Pooky Knightsmith: www.inourhands.com – webinars, videos and podcasts aimed at supporting professionals support young people's mental health.

Mental Health First Aid: https://mhfaengland.org – providing funded and paid for training for schools and youth services around supporting youth mental health.

Why Not Find Out? www.wnfo.org.uk – up-to-date information site on alcohol and drugs.

References

Adley, M. (2018) 'The Drugs Wheel' (online). Available at www.thedrugswheel.com (accessed 15 August 2018).

Atkinson, A.M., Ross-Houle, K.M., Begley, E. and Sumnall, H. (2016) 'An exploration of alcohol advertising on social networking sites: an analysis of content, interactions and young people's perspectives.' *Addiction Research and Theory 25*, 2.

Battleday, R.M. and Brem, A. (2015) 'Modafinil for cognitive neuroenhancement in healthy non-sleep-deprived subjects: a systematic review.' *European Neuropsychopharmacology 25*, 11, 1865–1881.

BBC News (2013) 'Talk to Frank: do anti-drugs adverts work?' (online). Available at www.bbc.co.uk/news/magazine-21242664 (accessed 12 July 2018).

Blackman, S. and Bradley, R. (2016) 'From niche to stigma – headshops to prison: exploring the rise and fall of synthetic cannabinoid use among young adults.' *International Journal of Drug Policy*, http://dx.doi.org/10.1016/j.drugpo.2016.10.015.

Boddington, N., McWhirter, J. and Stonehouse, A. (2013) 'Drug and alcohol education in schools (online).' Available at http://mentor-adepis.org/wp-content/uploads/2013/10/Drug-and-alcohol-education-in-schools-full-report.pdf (accessed 1 August 2018).

Bourdieu, P. (2010) (in translation) *Distinction*. London: Routledge.

Bowlby, J. (1969) *Attachment. Attachment and Loss: Vol. 1. Loss*. New York: Basic Books.

Briney, J.S., Brown, E.C., Kuklinski, M.R., Oesterle, S. and Hawkins, J.D. (2017) 'Testing the question-behaviour effect of self-administered surveys measuring youth drug use.' *Journal of Adolescent Health 61*, 6, 743–746.

Butler, J. (1993) *Bodies that Matter: On the Discursive Limits of 'Sex'*. London: Routledge.

Centre for Longitudinal Studies (2016) 'Children's mental wellbeing and ill-health: not two sides of the same coin' (online). Available at www.cls.ioe.ac.uk/news.aspx?itemid=4510&itemTitle=Children%E2%80%99s+mental+wellbeing+and+ill-health%3A+not+two+sides+of+the+same+coin&sitesectionid=27&sitesectiontitle=News (accessed 18 July 2018).

Charlie Waller Memorial Trust (2016) *No Harm Done film for professionals* (online). Available at www.cwmt.org.uk/resources (accessed 28 August 2018).

Cortese, S. (2016) 'Cardiovascular safety of methylphenidate' (online). Available at www.nationalelfservice.net/mental-health/adhd/cardiovascular-safety-methylphenidate (accessed 5 November 2018).

Daniel, B. and Wassell, S. (2002) *Adolescence: Assessing and Promoting Resilience in Vulnerable Children*. London: Jessica Kingsley Publishers.

Department for Education (2014) 'Mental health and behaviour in schools.' Crown Copyright.

Department for Education (2015) 'Counselling in schools: a blueprint for the future.' Crown Copyright.

Department for Education (2016). 'Standard for teachers' professional development: implementation guidance' (online). Available at https://www.gov.uk/government/publications/standard-for-teachers-professional-development (accessed 8 November 2018).

Department for Education (2018) 'New relationships and health education in schools (online). Available at www.gov.uk/government/news/new-relationships-and-health-education-in-schools (accessed 5 November 2018).

Department of Health (2015) 'Future in Mind.' Crown Copyright.

Department of Health and Department for Education (2017) 'Transforming children and young people's mental health provision: a green paper.' Crown Copyright.

Foucault, M. (1991) *Discipline and Punish: The Birth of the Prison.* London: Penguin.

Hanratty, J. (2017) 'Mindfulness in schools: what next?' (online). Available at www.nationalelfservice.net/treatment/mindfulness/mindfulness-in-schools-what-next (accessed 18 July 2018).

Hart, A., Gagnon, E., Eryigit-Madzwamuse, S., Cameron, J., Aranda, K., Rathbone, A. and Heaver, B. (2016) 'Uniting resilience research and practice with an inequalities approach.' *Sage Open,* http://journals.sagepub.com/doi/10.1177/2158244016682477.

Knightsmith, P. (2015) *Self-Harm and Eating Disorders in Schools: A Guide to Whole School Strategies and Practical Support.* London: Jessica Kingsley Publishers.

Knightsmith, P. (2016) *The Healthy Coping Colouring Book and Journal.* London: Jessica Kingsley Publishers.

Kutcher, S. (2017) 'Is mental malaise the psychological equivalent of obesity?' (online). Available at www.nationalelfservice.net/mental-health/depression/is-mental-malaise-the-psychological-equivalent-of-obesity (accessed 10 August 2018).

LeGoff, D.B., Gomez De La Cuesta, G., Krauss, G.W. and Baron-Cohen, S. (2014) *LEGO-Based Therapy: How to Build Social Competence Through LEGO-Based Clubs for Children with Autism and Related Conditions.* London: Jessica Kingsley Publishers.

Local Government Association (2017) 'Bright futures: our vision for youth services' (online). Available at www.local.gov.uk/about/campaigns/bright-futures/bright-futures-childrens-services/bright-futures-our-vision-youth (accessed 12 July 2018).

Local Government Association (2018) 'Marmot review report – Fair society, healthy lives' (online). Available at www.local.gov.uk/marmot-review-report-fair-society-healthy-lives (accessesd 20 August 2018).

Maddison, A. and Handley-Ward, N. (2018) 'Body image and image enhancing drugs' (online). Available at www.cwmt.org.uk/podcasts (accessed 10 August 2018).

Marmot, M. (2010) 'Fair Society, Healthy Lives: The Marmot Review' (online). Available at www.instituteofhealthequity.org/resources-reports/fair-society-healthy-lives-the-marmot-review/fair-society-healthy-lives-full-report-pdf.pdf (accessed 20 August 2018).

McDonald, S. and Tomlin, A. (2017) 'Mindfulness for young people: to meta-analyse or not to meta-analyse?' (online). Available at www.nationalelfservice.net/treatment/mindfulness/mindfulness-for-young-people-to-meta-analyse-or-not-to-meta-analyse (accessed 23 August 2018).

McKay, M.T., Sumnall, H.R., Harvey, S.A. and Cole, J.C. (2017) 'Perceptions of school-based alcohol education by educational and health stakeholders: "Education as usual" compared to a randomised controlled trial.' *Drugs: Education, Prevention and Policy* (online) DOI: http://dx.doi.org/10.1080/09687637.2016.1273316.

Measham, F., Morre, K., Newcombe, R. and Welch, Z. (2010) 'Tweaking, bombing, dabbling and stockpiling: the emergence of mephedrone and the perversity of prohibition.' *Drugs and Alcohol Today 10*, 1.

Mentor-ADEPIS (2013a) 'Social norms: the power of following the pack' (online). Available from http://mentor-adepis.org/social-norms-the-power-of-following-the-pack (accessed 1 August 2018).

Mentor-ADEPIS (2013b) 'Caffeine and energy drinks' (online). Available at http://mentor-adepis.org/caffeine-and-energy-drinks (accessed 30 August 2018).

Mentor-ADEPIS (2014) 'E-cigarettes and nicotine containing products' (online). Available at http://mentor-adepis.org/e-cigarettes-nicotine-containing-products-ncps (accessed 30 August 2018).

Mentor-ADEPIS (2017) 'School-based alcohol and drug education and prevention – what works?' (online). Available at http://mentor-adepis.org/school-based-alcohol-drug-education-prevention-works (accessed 30 August 2018).

NHS (2016) 'Mindfulness' (online). Available at www.nhs.uk/conditions/stress-anxiety-depression/mindfulness (accessed 23 August 2018).

NHS Digital (2017) 'Smoking, drinking and drug use among young people 2016' (online). Available at https://digital.nhs.uk/data-and-information/publications/statistical/smoking-drinking-and-drug-use-among-young-people-in-england/2016 (accessed 1 August 2018).

Ofsted (2013) 'Not yet good enough: personal, social, health and economic education in schools.' Crown Copyright.

Perkins, H.W., Craig, D. and Perkins, J.M. (2011) 'Using social norms to reduce bullying: a research intervention among adolescents in five middle schools.' *Group Processes and Intergroup Relations 14*, 5, 703–722.

Perry, Y., Werner-Seidler, A., Calear, A., Mackinnon, A., King, C., Scott, J., Merry, S., Fleming, T., Stasiak, K., Christensen, H. and Batterham, P.J. (2017) 'Preventing depression in final year secondary students: school-based randomized controlled trial.' *Journal of Medical Internet Research 19*, 11.

Porcellato, L., Ross-Houle, K., Quigg, Z., Harris, J., Bigland, C., Bates, R., Timpson, H., Gee, I., Gould, A. and Davies, A. (2018) 'Is it all smoke without fire?' Public Health Wales.

PSHE Association (2015) 'PSHE Association responds to new social mobility research' (online). Available at www.pshe-association.org.uk/news/pshe-association-responds-new-social-mobility (accessed 9 August 2018).

PSHE Association (2017) 'A curriculum for life: the case for statutory PSHE.' Available at www.pshe-association.org.uk/curriculum-and-resources/resources/curriculum-life-case-statutory-pshe-education (accessed 1 August 2018).

PSHE Association (2018) 'PSHE planning toolkit.' Available from www.pshe-association.org.uk/curriculum-and-resources/resources/pshe-education-planning-toolkit-key-stages-3-and-4 (accessed 5 November 2018).

Public Health England (2015) 'Promoting children and young people's emotional health and wellbeing.' Crown Copyright.

Public Health England (2018) 'Evidence review of e-cigarettes and heated tobacco products: executive summary.' Available at www.gov.uk/government/publications/e-cigarettes-and-heated-tobacco-products-evidence-review/evidence-review-of-e-cigarettes-and-heated-tobacco-products-2018-executive-summary (accessed 1 August 2018).

Rose, J. (2015) 'One theory all teachers with disruptive children should know about' (online). Available at http://theconversation.com/one-theory-all-teachers-with-disruptive-children-should-know-about-43561 (accessed 18 July 2018).

Sex Education Forum (2018) 'Our response to call for evidence.' Available at www.sexeducationforum.org.uk/news/news/our-response-call-evidence (accessed 1 August 2018).

Shelemy, L. and Knightsmith, P. (2017) 'Building resilience in the face of adversity.' In Bush, M. (ed.) *Addressing Adversity: Prioritising Adversity and Trauma Informed Care for Children and Young People in England.* London: Young Minds Trust.

Shmueli-Goetz, Y. (2018) 'Attachment (in primary school aged children)' (online). Available at www.annafreud.org/what-we-do/schools-in-mind/expert-advice-and-guidance/attachment-in-primary-school-aged-children (accessed 18 July 2018).

Stallard, P., Skryabina, E., Taylor, G., Anderson, R., Ukoumunne, O.C. and Daniels, H. (2015) 'A cluster randomised controlled trial comparing the effectiveness and cost-effectiveness of a school-based cognitive behavioural therapy programme (FRIENDS) in the reduction of anxiety and improvement in mood in children aged 9/10 years.' *Public Health Research, 3,* 14.

Stapley, E. (2018) 'Young people's perspectives on difficulties, coping and support' (online). Available at www.corc.uk.net/news-blog/young-people-s-perspectives-on-difficulties-coping-and-support-emily-stapley-explores-what-we-can-learn-from-headstart (accessed 21 July 2018).

Still, C. (2017) 'Using creative interventions to support young people's mental health' (online). Available at www.addaction.org.uk/blog/using-creative-interventions-support-young-peoples-mental-health (accessed 22 August 2018).

Underwood, A. (2016) 'School-based CBT for anxiety and low mood: the FRIENDS programme' (online). Available at www.nationalelfservice.net/treatment/cbt/school-based-cbt-for-anxiety-and-low-mood-the-friends-programme (accessed 10 July 2018).

Unilever (2018) 'The Dove Self-Esteem Project.' Available at www.dove.com/uk/dove-self-esteem-project.html (accessed 6 August 2018).

Werner-Seidler, A., Perry, Y., Calear, A.L., Newby, J.M. and Christensen, H. (2017) 'School-based depression and anxiety prevention programs for young people: a systematic review and meta-analysis.' *Clinical Psychology Review 51,* 30–47.

Zuboff, S. (1988) *In the Age of the Smart Machine: The Future of Work and Power.* New York: Basic Books.

Subject Index

academic achievement 104–5
acceptance, importance of 123–6
adverse childhood experiences 51
alcohol
    'continental approach' 65
    education around 67–8
    engaging parents 64–6
    imagery used 57
    statistical data 57–8
'anonymous' power 72–4
art activities 127–8
attachment theory 47–8
awkward questions
    from adults 118
    from pupils 113–4

body image
    activities 71–2
    and cultural capital 70–1
    image-enhancing drugs 80–3
    Mind and Body programme 83
Brighton and Hove (PSHE) 40–1

caffeine
    case study 91–2
    cultural acceptance of 88
    guidance around 87–8
    in over-the-counter medicines 87
    side effects 88
    see also energy drinks
CAMHS service model 34–9

cannabis 96
causes underlying behaviour 95
cognitive 'enhancers' (smart drugs) 90–1
colouring-in activity 126–7
contagion 79–80, 84
counselling services 22–3
'county lines' practice 48
cultural capital 70–1

depressants 95–6
distancing techniques 114–6
DNP 82
Dove Self-Esteem Project 78
drop-day model 29–30, 105–6
'drug triangle' 98–9
Drugs Wheel model 95

e-cigarettes 61–4
eating disorders 76–9
education professionals/health
    professionals gap 45
effects, of drugs 96
emotions, curiosity around 119
energy drinks
    case study 91–2
    effects at school 89
    purchase ban (under 18s) 89–90
    statistical data 88
ex-user speakers 112
external expert speakers 99–102, 107

'fight or flight' response 46
FOMO (fear of missing out) 59–60
Fraser Guidelines 117
friendships 55
funding cuts 37
'Future in Mind' report 15, 35

games, interactive 128–30
'gaze', the 74
gender as performance 74–6

habitus 70–1
hallucinogens 95–6
harm reduction delivery
    unintended consequences
        of 60, 97, 117
    younger pupils 118–9
HeadStart programmes 23
health professionals/education
    professionals gap 45
'health terrorism' 93–4

image-enhancing drugs 80–3
imagery
    alcohol 57
    in schools 61

journaling/writing 127–8
judgement, avoiding 123–6
Just Say No campaign 30, 39

ketamine 95, 96
knee jerk responses 80, 94, 97

language/terminology 10,
    16–7, 107–10, 120
'legal high' (NPS) 32, 94
LGBT pupils 77–8
life skills approach 32–3
listening, importance of 123–6

Local Transformation Plans 35

media
    extreme reporting in 93
    on fatal drug use 116
mental health
    clinicalising responses to 108
    language around 10, 16–7,
        107–10, 120
mental health education
    definition of 103–4
    drop-day model 29–30, 105–6
    'expert' vs 'referent' approach 111
    external expert speakers 99–102, 107
    lack of guidance for 33–4, 104
    safe environment for 112–4
    specialist teachers model 107
    tutor time model 106–7
    wellbeing-academic
        achievement link 104–5
mental wellbeing 16–8, 104–5
mephedrone 94
mindfulness 21–2
modafinil 90
monitoring progress 16

nitrous oxide 96
NPS (novel psychoactive
    substances) 32, 94

over-estimation tendency
    11, 19, 59, 60–1, 66
over-exercising 76–9

panopticism 72–4
parent engagement 64–6
PCEs (smart drugs) 90–1
peer pressure 59
performance, gender as 74–6
personal disclosure 112–6

piracetam 90
power
    'anonymous' 72–4
    'expert' vs 'referent' 111
progress, monitoring 16
PSHE
    in Brighton and Hove 40–1
    delivery of 28–30
    expansion of remit of 27–8
    ground rules for 112
    history of 25–6
    life skills approaches 32–3
    position within National
        Curriculum 26–7
pupil voice 15

questions (awkward)
    from adults 118
    from pupils 113–4

raising awareness, unintended
    consequences of 60, 80, 97
'referent' power 111
relationship and sex
    education (RSE) 103
resilience 49–50, 51–6
risk assessment 97–9
Ritalin 90

safe environment 50–1, 54, 112–4
safety plans 120–1
school
    as safe place 50–1, 54, 112–4
    see also whole school approach
school nursing teams 37
secure base, school as 54
self-harm 120–1
shock tactics 30, 39
slimming pills 82
'smart drugs' (PCEs) 90–1
smoking 61–4

'Smoking, drinking and drug use
    among young people' survey 19
social competence 54
social determinants of health
    adolescents 46–7
    overview 43–5
social networking sites 59, 73–6, 83
social norms approach 59–61
'something is better than nothing'
    approach 80, 94, 97
specialist teachers model 107
'spice zombies' 94–5
statistical data
    alcohol 57–8
    energy drinks 88
    'Smoking, drinking and drug use
        among young people' survey 19
steroids 81–2
stimulants 95–6
suicide 120–1

Talk to Frank campaign 31
targeted support 15–6
tea 87
terminology/language 10,
    16–7, 107–10, 120
tiers of delivery 36–8
Time to Change campaign 87
'Transforming children and young
    people's mental health provision'
    recommendations 11–2
trauma in childhood 51
tutor time model 106–7

vulnerability, talking about 121

wellbeing
    link with academic
        achievement 104–5
    mental (vs. mental illness) 16–8
    of staff 15

whole school approach
  curriculum 14
  green paper (2017)
    recommendations 11–2
  leadership/management 13–4
  overview 12–3
  parent engagement 14, 64–6
  policy ethos 16
  pupil voice 15
  school as safe place 50–1, 54, 112–4
  staff development 14–5
  targeted support 15–6
writing/journaling 127–8

Author Index

Adley, M. 95
Armiger, M. 119
Atkinson, A.M. 59, 75

Battleday, R.M. 91
BBC News 31
Blackman, S. 94
Boddington, N. 104
Bourdieu, P. 69
Bowlby, J. 47
Bradley, R. 83, 94
Brem, A. 91
Briney, J.S. 59
Butler, J. 74

Centre for Longitudinal Studies 17, 18
Cortese, S. 91
Craig, D. 61

Daniel, B. 49, 54
Department for Education 11,
    22, 26, 27, 29, 52, 103
Department of Health 11, 35, 40
Devon, N. 71

Foucault, M. 72

Handley-Ward, N. 81
Hanratty, J. 21

Hart, A. 52, 53, 54

Kelly, Y. 75
Knightsmith, P. 23, 56, 79, 126
Kutcher, S. 108, 109, 110

LeGoff, D.B. 127
Local Government Association 37, 44

McDonald, S. 21, 105
McKay, M.T. 64, 99
McWhirter, J. 104
Maddison, A. 81
Marmot, M. 43
Measham, F. 94
Mentor-ADEPIS 29, 30, 31, 32, 39, 48,
    59, 61, 88, 90, 97, 105, 107, 112, 117

National Curriculum 26
NHS 21
NHS Digital 19, 77, 94

Ofsted 26, 27, 29, 40, 104, 105, 107, 111

Perkins, H.W. 59, 61
Perkins, J.M. 61
Perry, Y. 23
Porcellato, L. 62

PSHE Association 26, 27, 32,
    40, 48, 104, 105, 107
Public Health England 26, 29,
    32, 39, 40, 48, 62, 105

Rose, J. 47

Sex Education Forum 29
Shelemy, L. 56
Shmueli-Goetz, Y. 47
Stallard, P. 22
Stapley, E. 23

Still, C. 127
Stonehouse, A. 104

Tomlin, A. 21, 105

Underwood, A. 22
Unilever 71

Wassell, S. 49, 54
Werner-Seidler, A. 22

Zuboff, S. 73